Entrepreneur Magazine's

startup

Start Your Own

e-LEARNING BUSINESS

Your Step-by-Step Guide to Success

Entrepreneur Press and Mike Hogan

E̲p̲
Entrepreneur
Press

Editorial Director: Jere L. Calmes
Managing Editor: Marla Markman
Cover Design: Beth Hansen-Winter
Production: Eliot House Productions
Composition: Ed Stevens

© 2004 by Entrepreneur Media Inc.
All rights reserved.

Reproduction or translation of any part of this work beyond that permitted by Section 107 or 108 of the 1976 United States Copyright Act without permission of the copyright owner is unlawful. Requests for permission or further information should be addressed to the Business Products Division, Entrepreneur Media Inc.

This publication is designed to provide accurate and authoritative information in regard to the subject matter covered. It is sold with the understanding that the publisher is not engaged in rendering legal, accounting or other professional services. If legal advice or other expert assistance is required, the services of a competent professional person should be sought.

Library of Congress Cataloging-in-Publication Data

Hogan, Mike
    Start your own e-learning business/by Mike Hogan.
        p.   cm.   —(Entrepreneur magazine's start up)
    Includes bibliographical references and index.
    ISBN 1-932531-23-8
      1. Employees—Training of—Computer-assisted instruction. 2. Employees—Training of—Data processing. 3. Organizational learning—Data processing. 4. Internet in education. 5. New business enterprises—Management. I. Title: Start your own elearning business. II. Title: E-learning business. III. Title. IV. Series.

HF5549.5.T7H5963 2003
658.3'124'02854678--dc22   2003064279

Printed in Canada

11 10 09 08 07 06 05 04   10 9 8 7 6 5 4 3 2 1

Contents

Preface vii

Chapter 1
Learning for a Better Life 1
A Degree of Confidence 2
Learning Goes e 4
What's *Your* Role? 5

Chapter 2
Entering e-Learning Markets 7
The Education Industry 8
Beware of Geeks Bearing Gifts 9
Where Do *You* Fit In? 10
What Do Your Students Want? 12
Tools for Schools 12
On-the-Job Training 13
Keep on Keeping Online 14
Brainstorming Your Business 15
To Market, to Market, to Market Research 15
Search and Research 16

Start Your Own e-learning Business

Chapter 3

Start-Up Strategies 19
Get the Idea? 20
Filling a Certifiable Need 21
Certifiably Different 23
Making a Middleman Market 24

Chapter 4

e-Learning Goes to School 27
e-Writing, e-Reading, e-Arithmetic 28
Homes Rule! 30
e-Learning on (and off) the College Campus 31
Who's In the Audience? 33
Generation Internet 33
No Failure to Communicate 34
The Other College "Kids" 35
Follow the Money 36

Chapter 5

Tuning Up Knowledge Workers 39
Thinking Corporate 40
Continuing Education: Now More than Ever 41
Looking Out for the Bottom Line 41
What Knowledge Workers Need to Know 42
Data-Driven Professionals 43
Train Without a Plane 44
Mixing the Best Blend 44
Custom Coursework 46

Chapter 6

Training the Information Professional 49
Taking the Long View 50
Playing It Safe 51
Did We Mention Certifications? 52
Pricing the Product 54
What's Hot 55
Ready, Able and Demanding 56

Chapter 7

Lifelong e-Learning 59
Kids Are Born to It 60

iv

Adult Fare 61
Seniors Go PC 62
Continuing Education Reborn 64

Chapter 8
Solid Foundations for Virtual Firms 67
Mission: Entirely Possible 68
Make Your Case to the Right Jury 69
Name That Firm 70
Brand Exercises 72
Lawyers and Tigers and Bears 73
Create a Full-Powered Plan 75
Be Sure to Insure 76
Where Credit's Due 76

Chapter 9
Putting Your Money Down 79
Penny Pinching 80
Down Home or Downtown 81
Home Base 83
Picks in Commercial Space 85

Chapter 10
Content and Delivery 89
Content Is King 90
Getting Beyond Text 91
Instruction Beyond Instructors 92
Resale Value 92
Grow Your Own 94
Making the Delivery 95
Staying In Synch—or Not 97
Who Can Teach? 97
Protect Your Property 99

Chapter 11
It's All About the Software 101
Working the Web 102
Find a Friendly Host 103
Tools for the Creative Process 104
Come Together 105

Ten Technologies of Tomorrow 108

Chapter 12
Finding the Finances 111
Who Are You Going to Call? 112
Put It on Paper 113
Show Me the e-Money 114
Real-World Rainmakers 115
Network and Network Again 116
Stretching Exercises 117
The Shoestring Stage 118

Chapter 13
Spreading the Word 121
It's an Ad, Ad, Ad World 122
In the Virtual World 123
Telling the PR Story 125
A Welcome Site for Customers 127
Getting Sticky 128
Show Your Stuff 129
Word-of-Mouth 130

Chapter 14
Failure and Success 133
Rocky Road 134
Yes, You Can 135
Don't Quit Until You Hit 136
You'd Be Surprised 137
First-Mover Advantage 138
Don't Forget the Check 139
What's an Entrepreneur? 140

Appendix
e-Learning Business Resources 143

Glossary 151

Index 155

Preface

We live in the Information Age. In no other time in history is the acquisition and appropriate application of knowledge so important or so challenging. The personal computer and the Internet not only make vast stores of information available, but they make that information essential to our personal and financial well-being.

No longer is the computer the domain of a geeky priesthood of geniuses in white frocks laboring long hours over arcane and complex programs. The personal computer is becoming as pervasive as the telephone or television. Children are introduced to it in elementary school. They soon master e-mail, report writing, Internet access, and dozens of other common applications that, not so long ago, were the exclusive province of technicians with million-dollar equipment.

The real value of a computer isn't that it can do a better job than an array of old tools such as typewriters and fax machines, although it can. Rather, the computer has become the key that unlocks vast stores of constantly changing information that have become the real currency of most of our career skills. The ability to navigate the Internet has become a professional necessity for most white-collar and many blue-collar jobs. On the lighter side, the computer also provides personal enrichment and recreation. There are no limits to its functionality, to the imagination of the people using it, or to your opportunities in opening up that functionality to help people learn.

Today, e-learning (computer-based learning) permeates every education level. You'll find it in teaching children and seniors, in undergraduate and graduate-level college classes, and in continuing education of every stripe right down to traffic school. It plays a major role in aiding organizations that must continually train staff at all levels. And it is the preferred mode of learning for the growing cohort of high-tech workers who must constantly hone their technical skills and acquire the certifications that signify that accomplishment.

Education in this society never ends. Keeping up with the latest information is vital. What you learned five years ago, three years ago, or even a year ago may already be obsolete, especially in the area of technology. So the days of putting away the schoolbooks after the college degree are long gone. Education must now be an ongoing process.

That's both a challenge and opportunity for the e-learning entrepreneur. You must run faster to keep up. But if you do, you can be assured of an ever-growing need for your services.

You don't need an educational background to be involved in education any more. The field is relatively open for anyone from any background who wants to provide instruction in almost anything—and to those who develop the infrastructure, content, and other supporting services necessary for delivering instruction. An educational background can help, but it doesn't seem to be a prerequisite for start-ups at any level of e-learning. The best candidates to start an e-learning business are the same ones best suited for other ventures—plain-old entrepreneurs with lots of imagination and persistence.

Your place in the e-learning industry is limited only by your imagination. It's an industry that barely existed a decade ago, and it will continue to grow and change in ways that can't be foreseen. Entrepreneurs have already come up with some truly ingenious entrées, and in this start-up guide we'll explore some of the ways successful entrepreneurs did it. But there are no cookie-cutter approaches. Many entries will prosper. Many will fail.

This book is the product of interviews with industry experts and educators, market analysts, and the founders of e-learning ventures large and small. We'll look at how successful e-learning entrepreneurs define their missions, how they raise money, how they approach marketing, and how they handle the 10,000 other tasks that the chief cook and bottle washer faces every day.

Throughout the book you'll find tip boxes with information on the industry, as well as helpful ideas and advice for running your e-learning business. An appendix is filled with resources for the e-learning entrepreneur.

You'll also hear about the role of entrepreneurs in general and e-learning entrepreneurs in particular. We'll cover the veterans' struggles and the lessons they have learned. Their experiences and observations can provide insight into the path on which you are embarking.

Good luck, do some good, enjoy the freedom of being your own boss, and make a few million!

1

Learning for
a Better Life

Knowledge is the coin of this realm. Unless you're a movie star, professional athlete, or perhaps the founder of a start-up company, what you know is far more important than just about anything else in the business game.

To hold your own in the marketplace, you've got to keep learning—everything from changing social norms to the latest management theories to mastery of technologies that didn't even exist a few years ago. That's equally true in boom times and bad times.

In this chapter, we'll look at the circumstances that make education so important in today's economy and how they open up opportunities for you, the entrepreneur.

A Degree of Confidence

It's increasingly difficult to keep up with the faster pace of U.S. business, the constant push for ever-higher levels of personal productivity, the use of ever-more-complex technology, and the obsoleting of not-so-old job titles. This forces us to become more knowledgeable and work smarter—and, in many cases, to prove that we're making progress via degrees and certifications.

At the beginning of the 20th century, if you had even a high school education, you could get a good job. After World War II, a high school education became a necessity. Through the 1960s, if you had a little college—not necessarily even a full degree, but some post-secondary training—you enjoyed an edge that would get you a white-collar job. Now, a college degree is just the ante you must have to gain meaningful employment—and ongoing education is a must-have for economic survival.

Do you really need a bachelor's degree to handle most entry-level jobs? Probably not, if you took introductory business courses in high school, know computer basics, and have some common sense. But an increasing number of companies require the bachelor's degree even for these jobs. Why should a company hire an accounts payable clerk without a business degree when there are so many people who have one willing to fill that position? Why should a company invest in someone who hasn't invested in his or herself? That person isn't going to stay an accounts payable clerk forever. When the time is right for advancement, it's better to have someone who has the necessary credentials—namely, a degree.

Additionally, job applicants often find it advantageous to show that they have some specific technical experience in the job for which they are applying. An increasing number supplement their college degrees with post-graduate work, technical certifications and specialty training such as management seminars.

If you get a professional degree—if you're a doctor or lawyer, for example—you're likely to make three and a half times what a high school

> ## Smart Tip
>
> U.S. corporations will spend over $2 billion this year on e-learning, according to market researcher Eduventures. Catering to corporations represents a home-run opportunity for an e-learning entrepreneur, simply because of the size of each deal. Selling a course to a corporation can touch thousands of employees and lead to follow-up sales. The sale, however, will not be quick.

dropout will. Get that high school diploma, and you're likely to tack another $7,400 onto your salary. A bachelor's degree? That's worth another $17,500 a year.

Once you've got a degree (or maybe an advanced degree), you'll want more education and training. That may involve another degree, certification courses, or just learning all the details of a particular task.

And corporations need to make sure their employees are up to speed on all job requirements. That may mandate technical training, guidance on meeting regulatory standards, or management courses on issues such as sexual harassment and hiring/firing. The corporate move into e-learning is buttressed by extensive research showing that the new technologies often can deliver learning just as effectively and at a far lower price than conventional methods can achieve—and do so far more quickly and flexibly.

Ongoing education can be as ambitious as getting your MBA. Or it can be very fine-grained. "A lot of the online training is just getting people familiar with Microsoft Word®," says John Dalton, analyst with Forrester Research, a technology analysis firm. "It's not high-level stuff."

Training can be refreshers on "basic" material, since "the basics" often change every year. For instance, software tools are constantly being upgraded, with new versions of Microsoft Windows® or Microsoft Outlook® as well as new tools for video-conferencing, Web page authoring or instant messaging. That gives you ongoing opportunities to sell CD-ROM tutorials or Web courses to audiences who officially

Education Pays

Here are the median incomes of full-time workers aged 25 and older by educational attainment.

Professional degree	$80,200
Doctorate	$70,500
Master's degree	$55,300
Bachelor's degree	$46,300
Associate degree	$35,400
Some college, no degree	$32,400
High school diploma	$28,800
Some high school, no diploma	$21,400

graduated years ago and even those who think they "know" Outlook. And this scenario is in no way limited to computer training, since society's entire body of knowledge is growing and changing.

Learning Goes e

The seminal event for e-learning was the explosive adoption of the Internet, which became a vital part of our lives almost overnight. Computer equipment had been applied to education for decades, but when everyone hooked those computers up to the same communication backbone, e-learning really kicked into high gear.

In one recent cover story, *BusinessWeek* identified education as one of five sectors that will be revolutionized by the Internet. There are more for-profit education ventures than ever before, but we've barely gotten off the ground. The Internet's ability to free teacher and student from the constraints of time and space and allow distance learning is by no means being fully exploited. Students now can learn at a time and place of their own choosing, at the pace they pick. Or they can enter virtual classrooms led by instructors and delivered by any means computers can support, including live video if their PCs and Internet connections can handle it.

These new technologies don't necessarily kill off older methods. The determination of which learning methods fit a given need depends on a complex set of preferences among teachers and students, and on requirements imposed by the content of the courses.

Welcoming Webinars

Why are corporations so eager to adopt "distance learning"? Here's an example from the software industry.

In the past, companies that sold sophisticated software solutions that required extensive training would pack up two or three people, some laptops, a handful of manuals, and take a road trip to visit new clients. They might spend days at each site, instructing each new client's employees on the various subtleties of their solution, trying to pack everything they needed to know into a brief session.

Now they can conduct those training sessions live, over the Web, without having to go on the road. With products such as WebEx (www.webex.com), "I can see streaming video," says Jack Rochester, analyst at the Delphi Group, a technology strategy firm. "I can look at PowerPoint® slides. I can chat. I can interactively write messages and ask questions. I can conduct an entire briefing remotely."

Regular classrooms aren't going away. Often, the most effective e-learning happens when combined with classroom teaching—often called blended learning. E-learning ventures have discovered that one-on-one contact with instructors is an important element of some courses or preferred by some students. For example, the 50,000-plus students at University of Phoenix Online can complete their entire graduate degrees online, including all administration, registration, and book buying if they wish. But the university also has developed a learning option in which students can meet for the first and last class of each course and complete the rest of their classes over the Internet.

Stat Fact
The median time on the job for the average worker is 3.5 years, according to the Bureau of Labor Statistics. A 22-year-old college grad will change jobs eight times before age 32.

What's *Your* Role?

E-learning overall is a multi-billion-dollar market, which we'll examine in detail in subsequent chapters. The e-learning economy includes everything from CD courses about computer basics to a community college's Internet classes on business skills to corporate virtual classrooms on esoteric engineering subjects to third-graders following a scientific expedition over the Internet. E-learning can be about anything from growing orchids to personal finance to driver education.

There really are no limits to the subjects that can be delivered. People have a growing appetite for topics and interests that once seemed far beyond their reach, and companies have an insatiable need to keep employees up to speed.

Similarly, you can pick among many roles in the e-learning economy. You can specialize in teaching businesses large or small computer basics, management techniques, or high-end programming skills. You might create guides that help employees understand their firm's idiosyncratic software, or interactive content that explains complicated products to customers. You can create Web sites that help middle-schoolers with their homework, or training that helps seniors tune their Internet skills. You can provide content or marketing help or technical services to other e-learning firms. You can resell products. You can broker classes on behalf of other businesses, recruit students, resell CD-based courses, or engage in other middleman activities in the e-learning economy.

Bright Idea
Idea capital—that's what a company needs more than anything to succeed and stay competitive. A company that lacks new ideas will soon go out of business. Education is the key to maintaining a large bank of idea capital. And you, as the e-learning provider, are the provider of the raw materials that eventually become that idea capital.

Stat Fact
No less than 92 percent of employees say the ability to work from home is an important factor when deciding whether to accept a new job, according to the career Web site True Careers (www.truecareers.com). They are likely to feel the same about the opportunity to learn from home.

There are endless variations in audience demographics, delivery methods, content and learning styles. E-learning is new and wide open. Your ability to mine these opportunities depends only upon how well your skill set and delivery abilities match with these opportunities. You aren't limited by government regulations, social norms, past practices, or competitive barriers to entry. The market opportunities are really only limited by your imagination.

2

Entering e-Learning Markets

Education is an industry in the fullest sense of the word, just like health care or automobiles or food preparation. E-learning is the hottest corner of it, with huge room for exploration, experimentation, development, and growth.

Photo© PhotoDisc Inc.

In this chapter, we'll give you an overview of the market, discuss how some e-learning entrepreneurs have approached it, and tackle the fundamentals of how you can go about finding your unique place.

The Education Industry

In many respects, the pursuit of knowledge—including pre- and post-secondary schooling, job training, technical training, and continuing education of all stripes—hasn't changed in decades. E-learning is just a new way of doing a very old thing, just as word processors and spreadsheets were new ways of satisfying established business needs at the start of the PC era. The new PC tools did revolutionize business and personal productivity—eventually, after a good deal of painful trial and error.

E-learning is following the same track. E-learning is a growing part of a thoroughly entrenched human institution with tremendous history and momentum. Teaching is teaching, and e-learning is simply a collection of new methods.

That's great news for you, the e-learning entrepreneur. This market opportunity is not just a flash in the pan. It's not the Macarena or Razor® scooters.

E-learning breaks into three main markets, with considerable overlap between them. First is educating children and young adults, which is one of the largest industries. Some $100 billion a year is spent on this market, figures market researcher Eduventures and this spending is only going up.

If you round up all the e-learning products, systems, and services, and include that share of technological infrastructure and administration that these educational institutions can attribute to electronic education, you have around $5 billion in revenues today, Eduventures estimates.

E-learning has insinuated itself into just about every part of this education segment. And it's growing much more rapidly than the larger education industry. In fact, annual sales for e-learning should more than double to $11 billion by 2005, reports Eduventures.

Stat Fact
The e-learning segment of both the U.S. corporate business skills and IT training markets will grow at a compound annual growth rate of nearly 37 percent between 2001 and 2006, according to market research firm IDC.

This doesn't count the second major education market—the corporate market, which involves the training of both knowledge workers and computer-savvy IT (information technology) professionals. These are long-standing training markets using many of the same traditional methodologies. Market researcher IDC sees these overall markets growing nicely through 2006. However, the e-learning segments of those markets will grow three times as fast, or more.

The third market, which is hardest to quantify, is personal learning for enrichment or enjoyment. Here, e-learning might be a CD-ROM that helps a second-grader learn math at home, or a Net course on genealogy, or an interactive guide to understanding your latest electronic gizmo, or an instructor-led virtual tour of the world's great art museums.

All these educational markets can overlap with electronic publishing. For instance, Professional Training Associates (www.protrain.com) in Addison, Illinois, delivers management training handbooks and newsletters to interested businesses over the Net.

Beware of Geeks Bearing Gifts

Multibillion dollar markets with a zillion niches get people excited, sometimes overly excited. Words like "revolutionize" and "paradigm shift" are tossed around. Before you buy into them, remember again the history of the Macarena and Razor scooters.

Why the discouraging words? For one thing, because there is always a lot of hype surrounding any new movement, particularly one heavily based on technology.

As an e-learning entrepreneur, you must ignore the hype. You must spend serious time learning the rules by which educators in your corner of the market play as opposed to simply assuming that your technology will rewrite the rules.

On a practical level, you must accurately comprehend the true nature of the particular opportunity on which you embark. That's tough because markets are always changing. You don't always get reliable news of macro-or micro-economic shifts until it's too late.

But education isn't a market that must be made; it must only be converted to e-learning. You have the advantages of a proven need. You are swimming downstream in just one tributary of a very large river. Don't mistake the tributary for the river.

Where Do *You* Fit In?

What do you want to do with the rest of your life? You need to make money, but after that, how do you want to spend your day?

You must brainstorm about how to match your interests, skills and temperament with the right market opportunities. To get the juices flowing, here are some common entrepreneurial "job" descriptions in e-learning. As always in e-learning, they may overlap.

- *Instructor-led online learning provider.* Students can access your education or training over the Internet whenever they want ("asynchronously"), or you can deliver real-time virtual classes via various communications technologies ("synchronously"). This often is referred to as distance learning since the participants need not be in the same room or even country. (Strictly speaking, distance learning also can be delivered outside the Internet, via satellite TV or even radio—or by non-instructor-led options including CD-ROMs and videotapes.) A background in education is a plus here, since you want to make your student customers feel that they are being served as well as if they were in a classroom. Your start-up costs are not small, since you must hire live instructors (at least on a contract basis). You also must create or (more likely) license a sophisticated delivery mechanism that gets content to your students over the Internet. Fortunately, you also may be able to create "canned" content based on these live courses.

- *Content provider.* You're the creator here. You specialize in developing the actual educational material; others may package and deliver it. You may use standard software programs or create your own specialized tools for this. Start-up costs can be relatively low, depending on the talent and technologies employed. (Video, for instance, can get expensive very quickly.)

- *Content publisher.* As a content publisher, you sell Internet courses, CD-ROMs, videocassettes, and/or old-fashioned paper books. You might create this material or buy it elsewhere; you may sell directly or through distributors.

- *Infrastructure provider.* You let other people worry about content and customers while you provide the base technology or services. You might provide incidental services meant to be used in conjunction

> **Smart Tip**
>
> One of the most in-demand e-training entrepreneurs will be the educational consultant who goes into a corporate environment to determine individual training needs and creates a curriculum that is specifically geared toward that company.

with e-learning courses, such as e-mail, bulletin board, chat room, and online databases. Or you might go all the way up to complete Course Management Systems or Learning Management Systems. Either way, we are talking about a full-on software enterprise with a substantial investment in technology, office space, and talent.

> **Bright Idea**
>
> Reaching people who want to get into information technology fields can be tough because they are so spread out geographically. You may be able to attract them through advertising in local periodicals serving college campuses.

- *Contractor.* You're a freelancer, or a company that specializes in some key component for e-learning. You provide content development, programming, instruction, technical support, or other services to companies that deliver learning. Your start-up costs are small, and so are your chances of massive growth.

- *Exam preparation site.* You provide a Web site where students can prepare for exams. The site could be oriented toward almost anything from an SAT to a driver's license. But these sites are particularly popular among IT workers preparing for certifications. You post dummy tests with sample questions that show what students can expect from the real exam. You also may provide interactive forums where students discuss issues, plus a wealth of related content. Your revenue model is primarily subscriptions with additional potential for advertisements and site referrals. You will need equipment comparable to other Internet opportunities.

- *Certification provider.* You provide training with a test that leads to certification in a professional area. Your biggest struggle will be in marketing; you must establish a brand or be validated by a large partner.

- *Corporate employment skills testing.* More firms are turning to outside companies to verify the skills of job candidates. This can easily be handled online, with results immediately delivered to the hiring manager. Additionally, job hunters can refer the results to other companies.

- *Web aggregator.* You act as a one-step shop for certain kinds of learning. This demands partnerships with e-learning providers and the creation of a fairly sophisticated e-commerce site, which is no walk in the park. You also must address the challenge of marketing the site.

- *Reseller and middleman:* This is a catch-all category of activities that can serve any or all of the e-learning audiences. Some firms resell courses, others provide consulting services for companies looking to build their training programs. Others customize content for various e-learning sites, and some run reverse Web auction houses where students can shop for classes. You also might provide news, analysis or market research about the industry.

Don't be hamstrung by these categories; they aren't absolute. While they're all challenging, none of these roles need be restrictive, and no one says you can't grow your organization to fill more than one. Find a need and fill it!

What Do Your Students Want?

Before you start marketing e-learning material, you must be clear about what kind of students you will serve—and what motivates those students. Here are typical motivations:

- Maintaining job skills
- Advancing skills, with certifications or degrees
- Learning basics of computers or other key topics
- Preparing for entry-level jobs
- Learning advanced technologies and procedures
- Achieving a degree
- Continuing college or post-grad education
- Learning about an interest
- Getting out of a traffic ticket by going to online traffic school (really!)

Tools for Schools

America's public school systems have bought into personal computers big-time. There's now about one computer per four children, and increasingly those computers are reasonably powerful and definitely connected to the Internet. Federal funding has bolstered this trend, and new or renovated schools often come with a computer infrastructure that would put many businesses to shame.

Schoolchildren routinely do research on the Net, and their classes may have electronic pen pals in another state or continent. High school students may take virtual courses with other students spread across the country. And educational researchers are continually investigating powerful approaches, such as using handheld computers to help children master math and science concepts.

But all this has not budged the meter tremendously on e-learning spending. Teachers understandably focus on classroom interactions, they (or their school systems) may be slow to adopt new technology, funds are limited, nonprofits provide many offerings for free or at low cost, and instructional material may be vetted by state-wide educational boards or the public at large. So, while a substantial market exists here, it's smaller and growing slower than you might expect, and selling into it is far easier if you've got experience with the educational market.

The situation is similar for charter and private schools, although funds may not be as much of a problem for many of those.

In contrast, the home-schooling market is much smaller but perhaps more open to e-learning, especially if it supports a particular cultural or religious approach to learning. Another hot area is in preparing students from any kind of school for nationwide standardized tests.

> **Bright Idea**
> Recruiters, especially those who specialize in high-tech jobs, may be a good source of customers. Consider giving them a commission for referring students.

On the college scene, e-learning has made greater gains. It's getting harder to find a college or university that doesn't offer at least some online education opportunities (often courses that are actually delivered through an e-learning aggregator). At many institutions, incoming students must buy a computer, and increasingly campuses are networked not just with conventional wires but with wireless networks. Instructor-led courses range from very simple asynchronous presentations of text and graphics (with a discussion forum) to computer-enhanced classes that are broadcast in video simultaneously to students in the United States and Singapore. Opportunities abound here—if you can find the right niche and fulfill its requirements.

On-the-Job Training

It's almost always cheaper to provide incremental training to an existing employee than to train a new one from scratch. Companies struggle to find ways to keep good employees and those in certain hard-to-find skill categories; that's true even in a recession. Employers have a strong incentive to keep moving lower-level employees up the skills ladder, offering in-house training programs that groom lower-level employees. This represents an obvious opportunity for an entrepreneur to provide in-service training sessions to business clients.

"The more open-minded organizations are increasingly looking toward their internal workforce, and redeveloping those individuals," reports Kevin Rosenberg, principal of BridgeGate, a recruiting organization in Irvine, California. Rosenberg forecasts a growth in companies "reinvesting in people so they learn new skills, tools, techniques, and technologies."

You might focus your efforts on large corporations or small businesses or something in between. You might offer general training or courseware, or customize material for each client.

"Whatever your approach or subject matter, don't lose sight of the end goal," says Darren Spohn, founder and CEO of Spohn Training (www.spohntraining.com), an IT training company in Austin, Texas.

"It's important that training focus on how the customer uses the technology," says Spohn. "You have to teach what it means to them—whether they be in sales, an engineer, or an admin person. How can they use it in their job?"

Corporations want to see details on the value you add and the return on their investment (quantified, if possible). If you can consistently show that, it's a rare company that won't have employees you can help. And increasingly, companies will foot the bill for outside training rather than build that capability in-house.

Keep on Keeping Online

Not long ago, if you wanted to learn something after graduation, you either picked up a book and taught yourself or you enrolled in a continuing education class at a training center or community college.

If you took a class, you drove there two or three times a week, sat in a classroom and soaked up knowledge as best you could. Time and space were probably more of a worry than tuition. As you got further along on the work treadmill, it became tougher and tougher to continue your education.

The Internet is what conquers time and space for e-learning, especially for individual learning. Entrepreneurial pioneers have been offering computer-based training for decades. But the Internet was their definitive "ah-ha! "moment.

"The old model that you learn once in your life, put the books away, and live on happily ever after has just gone away," explains e-learning pioneer Steve Shank, founder of Capella University (www.capella.edu), an online accredited university based in Minneapolis. "We have this new paradigm of so-called lifelong learning that is being driven by the fact that every day, all of us face change driven by globalism, competition, and the fact that technology is changing all the time. So people have to keep on learning, acquiring new knowledge and skills."

The need was there and growing for a long time, and continues to grow. Net-based e-learning addresses another part of the puzzle: the fact that people's lives are just

---

Tackling Tech Support

When you offer a Web course, who do your students call if they experience technical difficulties? If it's a question an instructor can answer over e-mail or maybe even the phone in just a couple of minutes, you may want to offer this as a value-added service at no extra charge. After all, most students will probably have friends who are in the same boat, and if you go that extra mile for them, they'll recommend your courses.

Beyond that, you should consider how you will coordinate with tech resources (such as a college's computer lab support group) or for-fee services if free ones aren't available.

"jam-packed" as Shank puts it. You can learn where you want, and when you want. You can gain whatever knowledge you need, and just that knowledge, and just in bite-size chunks if that's what you prefer.

"The benefits of e-learning are absolutely compelling," says Shank. "It's not just delivery of e-learning itself; it's also all the support services that surround the learning. The Web provides a great support structure to reach out and help the individual.

Brainstorming Your Business

So which is the right niche for you? Where do you fit in? The answer depends on a confluence of factors—your location, your background, your personal preferences, your business skill set, your financing, and, of course, where you see an opportunity.

Over the next several chapters, we'll explore the state of different popular e-learning markets in greater depth. But those observations will still be broad strokes. The discussion is just a backdrop for your individual opportunity, which you have to make for yourself. And you can't do that just by jumping in where the hype is loudest or even where money is being made.

Doing his business start-up research, Mark Carey, CEO of MySoftwareHelper (www.mysoftwarehelper.com), a training reseller in Tacoma, Washington, came to a crossroads where he had to decide whether to create e-learning courseware or sell it. "I decided to sell e-learning as opposed to create e-learning," he says. "I'm a sales guy, not a developer. I have 18 years of sales experience."

Figuring your strengths like this is one critical step. Another is to refocus the definition of the audience you've identified into a viable market. In many cases, the audience itself doesn't know it's being under-served, so you must raise the collective consciousness and "make a market." In fact, you could say that, whatever you eventually end up doing in e-learning, you will create that particular market.

And what role does technology play? Can you make a market by being the first e-learning entrepreneur on your block to videoconference with students wirelessly? You need to find technology that solves real problems—and you need to figure what you'll do when your rivals acquire similar technical chops.

Precision Information of Madison, Wisconsin, relies partly on a technical edge: Its unique database structure aids in customizing content for personal finance trainers. But Precision (www.precisioninformation.com) must keep figuring out what it will do for an encore. And so will you.

To Market, to Market, to Market Research

You need to look before you leap. Step one: Figure out what you want to do and research the market; or alternatively, research the market and figure what you want to do.

Realize, of course, that after you do your research, you may have to change your plan. Here's one striking example: The co-founders of Spry Learning (www.sprylearning.com) in Portland, Oregon, thought they'd be selling communication equipment to separated family members. But after doing some market research, they wound up developing courseware and instructing trainers how to teach basic computer skills to seniors living in retirement communities.

> **Smart Tip**
>
> A good source of e-learning market research and ideas is the American Society of Training and Development (www.astd.org). Membership costs $250 a year and opens up a wealth of studies and white papers, newsletters, and bulletins.

Market research is many things to many people. To outfits like Procter & Gamble or Coca-Cola, it means spending tens of millions of dollars on empirical surveys and consumer focus groups to find out if people respond to "lemony fresh" or need a tad more zing in their flavored sugar water. To others, it's looking for a product or service that they themselves want, and finding that no one seems to offer it.

Market research may be as simple as taking an informal poll of friends, family, and acquaintances about their continuing education needs. It may be as complicated and expensive as hiring a professional market research firm to do the legwork and prepare a report. (By the way: Try to hire a freelance market researcher if you can.) Or it might mean asking questions in education-related chat rooms, Web logs (blogs), or online bulletin boards.

Nothing beats getting to know your audience directly and working with it. That's how the co-founders of Spry Learning discovered they needed to redefine their product plans–by volunteering their time at senior centers prior to launching the company. In corporations, you might pick the brains of any executives, managers, or other employees who are willing to talk with you. In schools, you might ask a teacher to let you sit in on their classes or question students about what would help their studies. You might show them coursework you've developed to get some constructive criticism. You might even do some tutoring, to help get that reality check.

Don't forget the Internet. Both Spry Learning and MySoftWareHelper swear by the Net for market research. Whatever it is you're looking for, however parochial your need may seem to you, it's probably covered in spades on the Net. Carey spent six months reading white papers and investigating courseware companies over the Internet. "You can find anything online," says Devin Williams, co-founder of Spry.

Search and Research

It's up to you to figure out the right market approach, and then do it the right way to get the right picture. You can find a primer on market research in Chapter 1 in

Start-Up Basics. It has important source references like the U.S. Census Bureau (www.census.gov), where you can find demographic information that will help you draw a picture of your market.

Try to gain an understanding of what your potential customers need in the broadest sense. Yes, the conclusion of your research might be that there is a crying need for asynchronous courses to help people qualify for the Microsoft Certified Systems Engineers (MCSE) test. At the moment, there is; and it might be enough for you. But who knows how long that opportunity will last? Then what—what is the deeper need, the broader market?

Assuming you'd like to stay in business for more than a year or two, what will you do for an encore? What if your vision and/or skills cannot take you to the wider opportunities and enable you to keep pace as a hot market opportunity migrates to other software platforms? Your market advantage must be something deeper than just being another provider of generic courses or certifications—even if it's just having good business sense. In many ways, that's the best market advantage of all.

What Customers Pay to Play

Here are some samples among the wildly varying prices for e-learning products and services.

K-12 tutorial session	$25–$50/hour
Interactive CD-ROM for K-12 courses	$15–$40
Asynchronous online general interest course	$50–$75 per course
Instructor-led noncredit college course online	$40–$100 per course
Instructor-led college credit course	$500 and way up per course
High-volume corporate course on general business topics	$20 per student and way, way up
Interactive CD-ROM on business productivity or IT training	$40–$500
Multi-user network license for business productivity or IT training	$4,500–$10,000 per license
Interactive asynchronous course developed especially for a corporation	$5,000 and way, way up
Instructor-led course custom-developed for a corporation	$20,000 and up

Don't forget to find out who is competing against you. That shouldn't be too tough because they should be visible any place you could sell your products or services. Make a list and start building a profile of each. Sample their products or services if possible. Then figure out what they're not offering. There will always be people willing to pay more for something better. You just have to find them.

Market Research Checklist

Market research needn't be costly or time-consuming, and you can more than likely do it yourself. Here's a checklist to make sure you cover the basics.

❑ Loosely identify the type of individuals you want to target (such as seniors, career people, children, or other e-learning companies).

❑ Conduct your demographic and business research to determine if there are sufficient members of your target audience within your reach.

❑ Find out who else is targeting this audience, and make a list of your competition.

❑ Look at your competitors' brochures, advertisements, and Web sites. Determine what they're offering beyond the basic and what they're charging. List their pros and cons.

❑ Find an opening, a niche, a weakness, or some other way to differentiate your business.

❑ Put a brief description of your offering before some representatives of your target audience to see if they would be interested. Skip the sales pitch—just gather information about what kinds of training they're interested in and how much they would pay.

❑ Spend some personal time as close to your audience as possible.

❑ Adjust your initial impressions and redefine your market approach if necessary.

3

Start-Up
Strategies

Starting a business of any kind is challenging. But the depth and breadth of e-learning opportunities are such that you should have no problem finding a niche that suits your interests and financial resources.

You may start as a contractor working for a content provider, corporation or educational institution. Then again, you might invest hundreds of thousands of dollars developing a software product or an e-learning environment. You may fit in somewhere in between.

In this chapter, we'll detail some of the most established e-learning opportunities, so at least you'll know the paths most traveled. It's up to you to blaze your trail.

Get the Idea?

First off, you have to come up with the grand idea. That may be the product of a lifelong ambition. It may be the result of market research. You may be working in a related field and see an opportunity that just shouts out to you, even though no one else seems to get it.

Way back in 1987, John Clemons, now CEO of LearnKey (www.learnkey.com) in Orem, Utah, noticed that many people were having trouble getting up to speed on a hot selling word processing package developed by another local company, WordPerfect. A producer of educational films for the Brigham Young University Motion Picture Studio at the time, Clemons decided that the world needed an educational video of a WordPerfect expert providing step-by-step instructions on the software. Clemons began taping instruction sessions in his basement and marketing them directly to WordPerfect users. Now his company has e-learning partners worldwide and sells mostly to corporations.

Joe Saari, co-founder of Precision Information in Madison, Wisconsin, knew he wanted to be in business long before he knew what business he wanted to be in. It went all the way back to a childhood selling the produce from his vegetable garden door-to-door. By the time he had gotten an MBA in finance and was working as a consumer advisor for a large financial services company, he was positive that he didn't want to work for someone else all his life.

Saari always had several ideas incubating at any time. But his experience in the financial services industry showed him the need for a complete financial reference for experts and novices alike. Saari and his partners created a searchable Encyclopedia of Personal Finance online and on CD-ROM. Since 1999, Precision Information has helped more than a million people improve their understanding of financial topics.

Similarly, Sarah Chapman and Devin Williams of Spry Learning had talked about going into business together since meeting in college. Chapman graduated with degrees in economics and political science. After college, she headed up national accounts for specialty markets for one of the nation's largest book publishers. Williams collected a bachelor's degree in finance and a Harvard MBA, and became a financial analyst for a large investment banking firm.

The two wanted a business that leveraged their skills and technology and helped people. That brought them to senior centers with the idea of creating a communication device to help seniors stay in touch with their families. They soon realized that there was a real need to expand the horizons of seniors who became landlocked in their residential communities. Chapman and Williams set up a nationwide company that helps assisted living staff teach computer basics to seniors, and then delivers courses and other services over the Net. Spry Learning is now passing $4 million in annual revenues.

> **Smart Tip**
>
> **Tip...**
>
> In any business, you'll want to develop multiple revenue streams to soften the blow from changing economic conditions. For example, your primary revenue stream might be training courses. But you might also earn additional revenue by selling related products such as textbooks, software, or computer hardware.

Even if you follow an e-learning road that's well-traveled, there is always the opportunity to put your own unique spin on it. To be truly successful, you must offer something unique about your approach, your marketing, your cost structure, the quality of your service, or another key aspect that sets you apart from other providers. And you'll need to be flexible enough to reinvent yourself along the way.

There are a lot of different ways to get into the e-learning business. Each offers pros and cons. They require different types of skills and personalities. They also can require vastly different amounts of start-up capital. In each, it can take awhile before you get a good reputation and a network of customers.

To illustrate the range of e-learning opportunities, we'll provide details on two very different kinds of businesses below, including certifying IT professionals (a well-defined and well-established approach) and acting as an e-learning middleman (a burgeoning and loosely defined field).

Filling a Certifiable Need

There is a serious skills shortage in many technical areas, and certifications are a popular way for employers to differentiate among qualified and unqualified job candidates.

"Certification is no substitute for a university degree," says Doug Kendzierski, Assistant Vice Provost at the University of Maryland, Baltimore. "But the largest challenge for industry right now is to find a beating pulse with a propensity to succeed in a technical career track," he says. "The employment community is turning to the certification to differentiate between those with validated skills that are in the mainstream of employment, and those that are more of an employment risk."

From the student's perspective, certification offers a way to get up to speed in technical areas and to break into the high-tech job market quickly with some marketable, proven skills.

Bright Idea

Boost interest in your certification site the way they do at video arcades: Post the names of your top ten performers and the percentile scores for any student who asks. Satisfy their curiosity, and give them bragging rights and verifiable proof of excellence that they can use to enhance their prospects for promotions and new jobs.

While a degree in computer science may take four or more years and cost up to $100,000, a string of enabling certifications can be achieved in under six months and cost just a few thousand dollars. They can be pursued before—or, more likely—after landing a job. In the latter case, it's very common for employers to pick up some or all the tab for the training.

"What you get with IT certification is some immediate bang for your buck in terms of salary increase," says Amit Yoran, professor at George Washington University in Washington, DC, and co-founder and CEO of managed security company RIPTech, which was acquired by Symantec in 2002. "It's a skill set and a criteria that a lot of employers look for when filling technical positions."

Building Brainbench

While some organizations focus on training students to take certification exams approved by specific product vendors, others create their own certifications indicating successful completion of a course of study in a broader topic area, such as networking. Brainbench (www.brainbench.com) in Chantilly, Virginia, became the big kahuna of high-tech certifications over the Net virtually overnight. Founded by Mike Littman and two partners in 1998, Brainbench has more than a million registered users who have taken five million certification exams in 400 subjects.

Seeing a clear need for screening IT professionals in the workplace, Littman left the corporate world and established a Web site where employers could prescreen worker knowledge levels in high-tech subjects (no training, just testing) prior to hiring.

A year later, Brainbench was hearing from individuals that its testing compared favorably to IT certifications elsewhere, so it changed its marketing strategy to target high-tech individuals. The site did 1,000 tests its first month and now provides certification exams online and at testing centers around the country for any individual who enrolls—particularly IT credential-seekers.

Brainbench works both sides of the street. Students who take its exams can make their information public, giving potential employers an opportunity to search the Brainbench database for a short list of job candidates. For example, an employer could go in and find the top 10 percent of people who passed a network administration course in a city or state.

"An IT worker can't advance indefinitely without a university degree," adds Yoran. But many IT professionals pursue higher degrees after certifications have already landed them jobs. Fortunately, even advanced degrees can be achieved online now—and often in much less time than through traditional universities. In the meantime, employers generally recognize certifications as adequate evidence of technical achievement, and additional certifications usually lead to higher salaries and increased responsibilities.

Certification courses provide the ad hoc training high-tech pros need, and are necessary for the growth and advancement of even those who hold computer-related degrees. Employers want people with highly specialized skills that are not necessarily available at the university. A certification proves to a potential employer that a candidate has a specific set of proven skills, or knows how to operate a certain software package or hardware platform. A person with a bachelor's degree in computer science has acquired the theoretical framework. But a person with an MCSE certificate knows precisely how to build and run a Microsoft network, so he or she can walk into a company and hit the ground running.

> ## Smart Tip
>
> *Tip...*
>
> To certify others, you must be certified yourself. In the vendor-specific area, for example, Microsoft offers several trainer designations. For vendor-neutral training, CompTIA has its CTT+ certification. This designation shows that a technical instructor has gained a standard of excellence in training and is well-versed in at least one topic.

Certifiably Different

Certification facilities traditionally ran in brick-and-mortar classrooms. But increasingly, both certification training and testing are being delivered online—either synchronously or asynchronously or in combination. (For some courses, self-paced online training must be augmented with hands-on classroom sessions.)

Unlike skill training, which focuses on teaching a student how to use a particular application or do a specific task such as run a network, exam training is a cram session. Although the theoretical goal is the same—to teach a student a level of proficiency in a given subject—the end result of certification training is the ability to pass the exam and gain the certification. Training is, therefore, usually very focused.

Actually giving the exams is another potential business opportunity. You can focus on two types of certifications: vendor-neutral and vendor-specific. A vendor-specific certification prepares a student to understand and operate a specific vendor's technology. For example, if you earn an MCSE, you're prepared to run a Microsoft network. A vendor-neutral certification, on the other hand, goes more into the underlying theory behind the specific technology. If you have a vendor-neutral background, it becomes much easier to move among corporate clients who may have different technologies in place.

> **Smart Tip** _Tip..._
>
> While the prices of IT courses vary widely, there are no clearly definable differences in profitability for the trainer between a vendor-specific course like Cisco's CCNA or vendor-neutral content like a CompTIA I-Net+ certification. Most IT workers need both types of training for their resumes. For maximum traffic, offer a mixture of both.

Both types have value, both are popular, and some people prefer to take both.

Starting any kind of certification center requires a larger-than-average investment in infrastructure, especially if you need facilities for classroom training. Considering the physical plant, trained personnel, and high-level content, you could easily spend $250,000 to get started. But your chances of success are good. It's a market that isn't going away soon, although, curiously, there are no franchises in online certification as of this writing. For more information about certification, subscribe to the free _Certification Newsletter_ by visiting ITWorld.com, clicking on "Newsletters," and selecting "IT Certification." We'll have more details on IT training in general in Chapter 6.

Making a Middleman Market

Entrepreneurs are consummate deal-makers, and many make great middlemen.

Don't want to run an online training center? Don't think you can handle the rigors of running an academic organization? Looking for an e-learning opportunity that offers more leverage than classroom instruction, but not interested in creating coursework or e-learning software?

You can still take advantage of e-learning opportunities by providing services to other e-learning entrepreneurs. You can be a reseller, a broker, or facilitator that matches students and teachers, a consultant, an industry analyst, or broker of other industry information, or you can provide other products or services to support the industry.

There's nothing really new here. Every market needs people devoted to supporting the smooth flow of information and business transactions among different levels of service providers and their ultimate customers. In the parlance of the Internet at large, there are B2B and B2C revenue models, and middlemen support both. They are often necessary supporting players for other peoples' transactions.

In education, there are so many different courses and categories of courses, so many training organizations and certification bodies, so many prices and options to discover that consumers can easily feel overwhelmed. They may not know what sort of training and certification they really need, where to start looking, or how to differentiate between providers. The source of that guidance may take many forms: a phone-book-size printed guide, a specialized Web search engine, an e-learning Web portal, a course broker, or various combinations of the above.

Esoftsolutions (www.esoftsolutions.com), founded by Sheldon Arora in 1997, doesn't teach, it consults. The Plano, Texas, company is a comprehensive e-learning specialist and systems integrator that gets paid to tell a blue-ribbon list of corporate clients which coursework or Learning Management System is right for them.

On a somewhat grander scale, WorldWideLearn.com (www.WorldWideLearn.com) functions as a one-stop shop for electronic education for individual students. Founded in 1998 by Angela Lovett, World Wide Learn claims to offer the world's largest directory of educational services through its Web site. It provides information resources as well as links to hundreds of e-learning courses in 125 subject categories—everything from a Ph.D. to courses on wireless technologies, sales training, and aromatherapy. The menu is broad, but the Calgary, Alberta, company specializes in matching students to online universities and certification courses.

You're never limited to just one e-learning opportunity; and sometimes those who provide directory or brokerage services may teach as well. OneOnOne Computer Training (www.oootraining.com), a veteran computer training company in Addison, Illinois, hawks its own set of courseware, but concentrates on bringing parties together, negotiating deals, and earning fees in the process. Founded in 1976 by Lee McFadden to publish self-paced math instruction for schools, in 1981 it began developing computer tutorials. Today, it provides quick tips and just-in-time tutorials on different aspects of popular productivity software to thousands of office workers and more complex IT training courses in conjunction with online partners.

Similarly, DevX (www.devx.com) offers online training, but is more of an omnibus source of information and training resources for the IT community using newsletters, libraries, chat rooms, bulletin boards, and a variety of media. Founded by Jim Fawcette, the Palo Alto, California, firm maintains a database/online exchange of 30,000 IT white

---

It's Bid Business

A "reverse auction" is just what it sounds like: an auction turned around. Instead of consumers bidding against one another for something offered for sale, sellers bid against one another for the privilege of selling something specified by the consumer. In a training reverse auction, a student decides he or she wants to take a particular course, goes to a reverse auction portal, and puts out a request for bids with a few qualifications like time frame. Several vendors check the site and submit competitive bids to provide the course or courseware. The one that offers the lowest price gets the sale.

Over time, expect this to become a popular way for companies, and then individuals, to hunt for the best price for training content and courses.

Bright Idea

Ask every customer for a testimonial, and post these testimonials from satisfied customers on your Web site.

papers and various service providers. Additionally, DevX develops custom Web portals through which corporations can deliver "just in time" e-learning, expert tips, code libraries, collaboration tools, and premium content and services to their employees.

One thing students typically look for is financial assistance. IT courses are pretty expensive, although studies have shown that you're pretty well assured of reaping economic benefits as a result of gaining IT certifications. Servus Financial Corp. in Sterling, Virginia, looked at those two facts and decided to provide the temporary financing students need to complete their IT courses. Its IT Skills Loan Web site (www.itloan.com) works both sides of the street, with programs to help both students and training centers work out their training financing. It arranges financing from $3,500 to $20,000 with seven- to ten-year repayment periods, and will even finance the purchase of necessary hardware.

NAPA Auto Parts is a car parts manufacturer and operator of the nationwide chain of more than 6,000 auto parts stores and 11,000 NAPA service centers. It also happens to operate a very sophisticated online learning center. The NAPA Institute for Automotive Technology (www.niat-training.com) conducts online training sessions for more than 9,000 local repair shop staffers and independent automotive technicians annually. The site operates in conjunction with NAPA's long-running classroom training program.

Traffic monitoring is another unusual opportunity—a role that sprang up with the interplay of Internet-oriented businesses. The thousands of e-learning Web sites have various referral programs among them and need an independent third party to help track, escrow, and facilitate the payment of commissions that are supposed to flow among them. One such tracking network is Commission Junction (www.CJ.com), which monitors the traffic among sites and 100 percent of online transactions around the clock. The Santa Barbara, California, firm was founded in 1998 by Per Pettersen and Lex Sisney. Imagine the time involved in tracking down and resolving commission mistakes without these types of escrow services. (PayPal, an online escrow company and another example of a necessary middleman, was so crucial to the operation of the hit online auction site eBay that eBay bought the company.)

To sum up: You may start off in rather traditional areas of education, but your opportunity is limited only by your own ingenuity and skills.

4

e-Learning
Goes to School

It's no surprise that e-learning has made huge inroads in the classic learning centers: K-12 schools and colleges. E-learning also plays an ever-greater role in the fast-growing home schooling movement.

E-learning's progress is most visible publicly in colleges. Traditional colleges and community colleges are deep into e-learning, and the online or virtual college has gained surprising popularity. These institutions are both competition and partners for e-learning entrepreneurs. Even if you aren't starting your own electronic college, the ones in existence can be customers for your content or software. Likewise, college campuses offer resources to entrepreneurs—classrooms, student connections, and marketing vehicles.

In this chapter, we'll look at opportunities in schools, starting with elementary and secondary schools.

e-Writing, e-Reading, e-Arithmetic

"The United States has done a pretty good job populating K-12 classrooms and libraries with computers. But there is a disconnect between the hardware and the children who use it," says the Pew Internet & American Life Project, which recently studied the interaction between kids and computers.

Pew gives schools an F in designing coursework and in providing computer usage basics. The same teens and preteens who can handle a joystick better than an F-14 fighter pilot have trouble in efficiently navigating both the PC and the Internet. One big problem, reports Pew, is that they haven't learned to touch-type. Another is that while they may be expert at certain computer skills like downloading MP3 audio files, there are vast gaps in their knowledge of "useful" computer skills and features.

Unfortunately, that's also true of teachers, according to research by Market Data Retrieval (MDR), a provider of marketing information to those who would like to crack the education market. According to MDR, 51 percent of schools report that 50 percent or more of their teachers are at the intermediate computer-skills level. Just under 25 percent put the majority of their teachers at a beginner level. Only 10 percent say the majority are at an advanced level.

On an up note, schools are gaining more of the latest technologies, including laptops, wireless networks and DVD drives. Funding for hardware remains strong, in part because of initiatives like the federal Elementary and Secondary Education Act. K-12 classrooms receive about $5 billion annually in tech resources. But schools are very restrictive in how, where and when the equipment is used.

Because of this, teachers are often reluctant to assign computer-related coursework for fear that children who don't have access to PCs at home also can't use PCs effectively on campus.

They could be right. While there are more computers at school, getting sufficient screen time is something else again, reports Pew. Middle school and high school students move from place to place and from teacher to teacher during the school day.

Only a brief period is spent with access to Internet-connected computers. While vastly improved in recent years, the student-to-computer ratio is still 4-to-1, according to MDR. How efficient would you be if you shared your PC with three other people?

> **Bright Idea**
> Why not mix education with pleasure? Start an Internet cafe targeted at teens doing homework. Don't forget to offer some supervision and take some sensible precautions.

Additionally, research activities often are stymied by restrictive access policies and content blocking and monitoring filters designed to protect kids as a result of the federal Children's Internet Protection Act. While some truly dangerous people lurk on the Internet and child safety always needs to come first, the approaches can raise problems.

"Our computers at school are all protected," one high school boy told Pew. "You can't send things or save things. You can't use the 'right click' or the 'Start menu,' so it's a waste and a hassle."

Unsurprisingly, Pew found that interest in computers is high among kids. More than three out of four high school and middle school students use the Internet regularly. Some use it to research school assignments, confer with classmates, and get papers completed. Pew reports that students said that many students share tips about useful Web sites, chat about class projects and tests, and even set up Web sites.

A combination of at-home access and keen interest in the Internet makes young people excellent e-learning candidates. But how can you replace video games with learning? And how do you keep kids interested in your e-learning offerings?

One way is by linking them with hands-on activities, which fits well with the latest educational thinking. According to a study by Rockman ET AL (www.rockman.com), a technology and consulting firm, elementary school students learn better when teachers link curriculum to hands-on projects—building models, designing buildings, or depicting living environments. Students are better able to visualize and assimilate a wide variety of subjects—not just science and social studies but math and language arts—if they feel that they are "discovering" knowledge rather than repeating it. E-learning can help.

Among successful players in the K-12 market, LearnStar (www.learnstar.com) in Dallas partnered with local computer resellers to bring laptops and wireless networks to elementary schools. The payoff is the interactive, quiz-style activities that LearnStar has designed to enhance learning, increase student motivation and, according to the company, increase students' standardized test scores by nearly 38 percent.

Kumon Math and Reading Centers (www.kumon.com) in Teaneck, New Jersey, which offers supplemental education after-school from more than 1,300 franchise locations nationwide, offers a blend of e-learning and more traditional methods to teach the youngest children reading readiness skills. That includes listening to reading CDs, games using alphabet boards, posters to sound out letters, singing, and flash cards. *Entrepreneur* magazine ranked Kumon as the fastest-growing franchise nationwide in its 2002 Franchise 500.

America's schoolchildren need help with math, reading and everything else they need to know. And where there's a vacuum this size, entrepreneurs will fill it.

Homes Rule!

Nearly two million students are being home-schooled throughout the United States today. It's a grass-roots reaction to declining test scores in public schools, local increases in violence and drug use, and concerns about peer pressure and mass culture.

Home-schooling opens up interesting opportunities for entrepreneurs. Who supplies the course materials for home-schooling? And how do parents get trained to school their kids? Who helps them with academic record-keeping, college and career counseling for their teens, and all those soft issues like discipline and fostering peer interaction with other kids?

Colleges will accept home-schooled youngsters, but they may have additional hoops to jump through. Who will help them? Who will point them to additional opportunities like Jones International University (www.jonesinternational.edu) in Chicago, a fully accredited online university that lets home-schooled students take college-level courses prior to high school graduation?

The National Home Education Research Institute and various other nonprofit support groups provide curricula and other help for parents who choose to home-school. However, they hold no monopoly on the activity. It's no different than many areas in our economy in which certain people have developed an expertise in what anyone could do for themselves. Home-schooling is custom made for service-oriented e-learning entrepreneurs.

Type "home-schooling" or "homeschooling" into any Internet search engine, and you will turn up a wealth of home-schooling Web portals that can tell you everything you need to know about the subject and give you a few moneymaking ideas.

> **Bright Idea**
> The Hobby Industry Association offers educational project sheets with materials to help you incorporate hands-on projects into coursework. They are available from (800) 645-7651 or www.hobby.org.

Think about it: Who would be more amenable to downloading e-learning content or resources than parents who are home-schooling their children? You can deliver courses or other resources for kids, give elementary education classes for parents, publish a home-schooling e-zine or newsletter, run a homework chat room, or establish a Web portal for other home-schooling service providers.

e-Learning on (and off) the College Campus

Post-secondary e-learning is still dominated by traditional colleges and universities. After all, they've pretty much owned the education franchise for a few hundred years. But that's changing. The market is opening up in no small part because education no longer has to be restricted to a very expensive campus. In fact, it can't be.

Demand for education is outstripping the ability of the traditional educational establishment to build new campus facilities or to support the number of students crowding onto the campuses they now have. The disparity is particularly acute among state-funded colleges and universities. It's most severe among the nation's 1,100 community colleges—many of which must accept all students who apply but are not guaranteed corresponding budget increases.

During and after recessions, enrollments typically go up as laid-off workers join college-age students, even while public budgets get squeezed. Rising tuition at four-year institutions is adding to the pressure on low-priced community colleges, reports the American Association of Community Colleges. This is the acceleration of a trend that has been building for a decade.

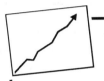

Stat Fact

Most colleges and universities (84 percent) operate a distance learning program, with nearly half these schools offering accredited degrees over the Internet, according to market research firm Market Data Retrieval.

Head of the Board

The Blackboard Learning System from Blackboard Inc. (www.blackboard.com) in Washington, DC, is a fixture on many college campuses, as well as in corporations and some K-12 classrooms as well.

An interactive learning environment with bulletin board, e-mail server, and chat room, Blackboard enhances the classroom experience and streamlines academic logistics.

Among other benefits, such "course management systems" from Blackboard and rivals such as eCollege and WebCT can boost idea exchange with constantly evolving asynchronous online dialogues. They provide a ready record of student-teacher and student-student interaction. This can create dynamics not always possible in regular, oversubscribed classroom courses.

Stat Fact

Enrollment at U.S. colleges has hit 16 million and will grow steadily for the next decade, according to the U.S. Department of Education's National Center for Education Statistics. Almost a half million international students enroll in U.S. bachelor or graduate programs annually.

Combine that with the sheer growth in the number of people pursuing sundry other types of continuing education—everything from traffic school to the pursuit of a hobby or the acquisition of advanced degrees or professional certifications. Clearly, the classic school can't do it all. The proliferation of strictly online universities and other e-learning ventures is proof of that. The University of Phoenix Online (www.uophx.edu) alone claims more than 50,000 students in the United States.

Traditional universities tend to focus on young adults with extension or community outreach programs extending their charter into older learners in the vicinity. Many of the dedicated electronic colleges, on the other hand, reach out primarily to older, working adults.

A certain segment of the population postpones higher education in favor of entering the workforce after high school. Older learners typically have time constraints that teens and 20-somethings don't: full-time jobs and families. E-learning in general, and distance learning in particular, can help.

E-learning modalities invaded traditional degree programs long ago. Naturally, institutions of higher learning have always been primary venues for training in every type of technology—from computer science to engineering degrees of every kind to generalized computer education provided as part of degree curricula or, perhaps, to the entire community through college extension programs.

Today, there is no college-level class to which e-learning techniques can't be applied. It would be hard to imagine a bachelor of science program nowadays in which computers were not central. Bachelor of arts programs would lag only a little. In fact, it's the rare subject in the traditional brick-and-mortar campus, in the social sciences or even fine arts, that doesn't involve Internet research. Many add multimedia tools, teacher-to-student e-mail, or Internet chat sessions, or the use of Web sites for posting class information, curricula, or lectures.

Colleges have invested heavily in infrastructure for this. For example, 45 percent of institutions report that their students can tap into a wireless network for mobile computing, reports MDR.

No one has to tell a student how a computer can help smooth the path to a degree.

Fun Fact

Not only are 100 percent of colleges and universities connected to the Internet but also 64 percent of classrooms are connected, according to market research firm Market Data Retrieval.

This is a post-Nintendo generation, and most grew up with a game controller in their hands and access to a PC at home or school. A recent Pew Internet & American Life Project found that one-fifth of college students first started using computers between the ages of five and eight. By age 18, all had used one.

Also, by now, middle-aged workers seeking to improve their resumes have gotten the message, too.

Bottom line: You don't have to sell students on the benefits of learning with computers. But how do you focus on the segment you want to reach, and how will you reach them?

Who's In the Audience?

Whether you are targeting college-age students in traditional institutions or jobholders working toward a bachelor's or advanced degree, the audience is relatively affluent.

The 15 million-plus U.S. college students aged 18 to 30 have discretionary buying power of nearly $200 billion a year, according to a recent 360 Youth/Harris Interactive College Explorer Study. (360 Youth is a youth marketing group, while Harris Interactive is a leading Web market researcher.) Parents and scholarships help with tuition. While college is often a financial struggle for students and parents, as a group they are not a downscale bunch.

Workers returning to college have jobs, of course, and, while it would be a mistake to characterize any working family as rolling in it, money is not really the main problem they face returning to school. A high percentage of employers are only too happy to underwrite an employee's continuing education.

There is a market, deep and broad; and the people who populate it have one thing in common—a limited amount of time to get the job done. E-learning, particularly distance learning, offers both groups a new level of flexibility and the chance to optimize their most precious commodity—time.

Generation Internet

Today's college kids are more sophisticated about technology than any previous generation. They are well-equipped with PCs and other devices, and have demonstrated knowledge about them and strong preferences for certain brands. Ninety-two percent own a computer, 69 percent own a cell phone, and many have handheld computers. According to a recent 360 Youth/Harris Interactive College Explorer Study, approximately 93 percent of the 15.6 million U.S. college students aged 18 to 30 access the Internet regularly, making them the most connected segment of the population.

They are quick to invest in new technologies, with two-thirds of students interviewed saying they either are among the first to buy a new gadget or device, or will soon after seeing their peers try it.

Why Students Go Online

Students report they use the Internet most often to:

Communicate socially	42%
Engage in work for classes	38%
Be entertained	10%
Communicate professionally	7%
Not sure	2%

Source: Pew Internet & American Life Project College Students Survey

College students have a relatively large amount of free time that could be used to advance their education. Including weekends, they have an average of 11 hours per day of unscheduled time when they're not sleeping, working, studying, or attending class, reports the Harris Interactive Study. But schoolwork does not necessarily drive their interest in technology (big surprise!).

No Failure to Communicate

When you examine how young adults use the Internet, the themes of recreation and communication jump out loud and clear.

When college students aren't talking on their cell phones, they are communicating via computer. The Pew research found that two-thirds have at least two e-mail addresses, almost three-fourths check e-mail at least once a day, and a quarter use instant messaging every day.

Almost three-fourths turn to the Internet for research more often than the school library, and almost as many stay in contact with professors via e-mail. When asked their motivation, students don't report using the Internet to get better grades or for the joy of learning. The Internet is just a way to get their work done more quickly.

In terms of recreation, the Pew study found that 60 percent of college kids have downloaded music files from the Internet. Downloading courseware and interacting with e-learning sites should be no problem.

Another popular pastime is interactive Web games. This is a major shaper of young adult experience and behavior. DFC Intelligence, a San Diego-based game industry firm, estimates that the number of online games being played will grow by a factor of six by 2006, and the number of people playing them will more than double, reaching 114 million.

While that sounds like a colossal waste of time, it builds proficiency with the computers that may pay off in e-learning—especially, courses and simulations that have some aspects of games. Gaming also fosters a familiarity, maybe even a preference, for electronic communications and sociability.

This level of skill and comfort can be transferred directly to the workplace, and a key resource for e-learning entrepreneurs to tap.

However many hours there may be in a day, there is no student of any age who isn't interested in taking online courses in convenient (or unscheduled) time slots, from home or a dorm room.

Also, recent growth in the number of college students is straining traditional college resources as prosaic as parking spots. In many colleges around the country, students may have high annual fees for scarce parking spots, and then end up walking long distances from street parking to class anyway.

Here's another incentive: MDR reports that roughly half of distance learning courses do not require students to purchase textbooks or supplemental materials.

But despite all these potential advantages, Pew reports that the traditional college students (18 to 22 years old) it studied show little interest in abandoning the classroom and taking courses online. So far, only about 6 percent of students have taken online courses for college credit.

> So far, only about 6 percent of students have taken online courses for college credit.

And only slightly more than half thought online courses were worth their time. Half of the students who took an online course said they believed they learned less from the online course than they would have from the classroom experience.

But that's good news for you: The market is barely penetrated, and current providers are not doing the job. If you can, and the word begins to spread, you have a wide-open playing field in the college market.

The Other College "Kids"

Not everyone finishes college in their early 20s. There are a lot of back-to-schoolers working at companies looking for undergraduate and graduate degrees. In fact, according to the National Center for Education Statistics, less than a quarter of U.S. adults aged 26 to 64 have a college degree.

If you choose to target back-to-college workers, you will be addressing an obviously more world-wise audience, and a more motivated one (no offense, kids). It's also one that has more problems completing their college education than young adults, time pressures being principal among them.

Stat Fact

According to the National Center for Educations Statistics, the fastest-growing group attending higher education institutions are working, part-time students older than 25, termed "learning adults."

Among the three-quarters of those surveyed by the National Center for Education Statistics who haven't completed college, the most commonly cited barriers include the fixed hours of institutional learning, prohibitive attendance requirements, lack of child care or other family support, and unfocused course information. Problems—or a huge market opportunity?

Conspicuously absent from that list is financial problems. Now, money is always a problem to some degree, but there are untold millions in education underwriting funds from the companies that employ these individuals that are going unused. NCES surveys indicate that 95 percent of U.S. employees with education benefits tied to their employment don't take advantage of this opportunity. Part of the reason is that students usually have to pay tuition up front and are only reimbursed by their companies.

But the principal problem for these students is time. Interestingly, of the 5 percent of workers who do take advantage of company educational benefits, says NCES, more than 85 percent now pursue their education at least partly online.

While NCES studies show that college-age students are taking increasingly longer to get their degrees, working students are all about getting it done. Who wouldn't be when working days and going to school on nights and weekends?

Not surprisingly, this audience is very amenable to synchronous and asynchronous e-learning. Merrill Lynch estimates that more than 2.2 million individuals take college-level courses online.

Also, don't forget those serving their country; a huge and highly motivated group. Saint Leo University (www.saintleo.edu) in Saint Leo, Florida, claims to be the largest provider of complete online degree programs for the U.S. Army, with more than 38,000 enrollments in 14 regional centers on military bases and community colleges, and that's just one branch of service.

Follow the Money

Colleges and universities comprise a massive market for e-learning services. MDR says that colleges continue to increase their spending on hardware, software and a wide range of technology-related services, and that it now runs about $5 billion annually.

"Course management systems, which provide a common user interface for professors to construct and deliver courses, are becoming commonplace on college campuses; wireless networks are making headway; and the majority of schools report that they now operate distance learning programs," says an MDR report. The report concludes that the evolution of the digital campus "continues at breakneck speed."

Content and teaching time aren't the only things entrepreneurs can offer colleges. Someone needs to provide, and keep providing, those course management systems (CMS), which make it easy for instructors to construct and deliver online courses.

Some of the most popular CMSs come from Blackboard (www.blackboard.com), eCollege (www.ecollege.com), and WebCT (www.webct.com). They offer the infrastructure required to deliver courses with all the necessary features (such as bulletin boards) in a well-integrated user interface. They also can simplify easy integration into the institution's own systems for online registration, grade reporting, and other administration

> ## Fun Fact
> America's college-age students each have about $287 a month to spend after tuition and room and board, according to 360 Youth/Harris Interactive College Explorer Study. What do they buy? About $11 billion worth of beverages and snack foods—more than twice what colleges spend on e-learning.

Doing a Bisk Business

What's the biggest name on the virtual campus? Yale? Harvard? Phoenix? How about Bisk Education (www.bisk.com)?

Nope, the Tampa, Florida, company hasn't appeared in any New Year's Day bowl games. But as a result of a consortium of online universities it has built (www.universityalliance.com), this e-venture can claim to be one of the nation's largest providers of accredited online college degree programs. Bisk works extensively with Fortune 500 companies who are more than willing to underwrite the continuing education of their employees.

Founded in 1971 by Nathan Bisk, the company pulls out all the stops on e-learning technology, including streaming video and audio lectures you can view as many times as you like when you like and virtual office hours in chat rooms where students can discuss lectures with their instructors. Web pages are used for displaying a syllabus, weekly assignments, and grades. Student interaction is fostered with chat rooms, message boards, and e-mail.

Among the universities participating in Bisk's University Alliance are St. Leo, Villanova, Regis, Tulane, and the University of South Florida in Tampa. Student bodies have been recruited from American Airlines, Boeing, Dell, FedEx, Home Depot, Hewlett-Packard, NASA, and Sony Music Entertainment.

> **Bright Idea**
> Don't miss the opportunity that a fast-growing Hispanic community offers to specialize in Spanish-language e-learning.

tasks. CMSs, which are also used extensively in corporate and even in K-12 education, can be bought with existing courses.

As CMSs expand their functionality, they start to turn into learning management systems (LMSs), which are sometimes described as complete "ecosystems" for e-learning. These systems integrate CMS with other software tools for solving all the learning needs of an enterprise (educational or other). Again, a college may want help in acquiring, setting up, and running an LMS.

Overall, "e-learning enables new opportunities for post-secondary educational institutions to fulfill their missions more effectively," explains Adam Newman, research director at Eduventures. "E-learning has not fundamentally changed the missions of these institutions, however. Rather, it has enabled the implementation of new strategies that are transforming the way teaching and learning occur."

Some institutions are moving a limited number of classes to a distance learning format as pilot programs, while others are going full-speed ahead with degree programs that can be delivered to students at remote locations, many of them at the graduate level.

Obviously, electronic colleges like Jones University and University of Phoenix Online are in the latter camp. They are pushing distance learning to the limit. They also may reach out beyond knowledge workers. Jones, for example, has an outreach program to provide advanced placement to home-schooled teens. As always, there are no walls in entrepreneurship.

5

Tuning Up Knowledge Workers

Training corporate workers, or providing courseware or a teaching platform to corporate training programs, is a huge market. Businesses have obvious training needs, they can afford to pay substantially, and they typically buy in volume. A license for hundreds of seats for just one course isn't unusual, according to LearnKey of Orem, Utah, whose reseller franchisees carry its broad menu of courseware to corporations around the world, and in some cases, offer support and training.

Competition is fierce in this market. It requires a high degree of polish, solid financing, strong sales and marketing skills, and the ability to deal with long sales cycles.

In this chapter, we'll talk about corporate training.

Thinking Corporate

Corporate opportunities vary. You can train workers on general business skills, management techniques, applications, and processes that are unique to their industry or their company, and in general use of computers. There's also a very large and very established market for specialized training for IT professionals, which we'll cover in the next chapter.

John Dalton, a senior analyst at Forrester Research, recently interviewed 40 training managers and chief knowledge officers at Global 2500 companies. "Of those 40, 39 already had online training initiatives up and running," Dalton reports. "They're completely jazzed about it, primarily because it saves them money."

One reason you can be jazzed about business training is that the delivery mechanisms can be quite sophisticated in corporations. Most companies have robust desktop equipment and high-speed Internet connections. They aren't constricted by the slow dial-up accounts that many home subscribers still endure.

That's true even for telecommuters, a rich potential market for e-learning. The proliferation of telecommuting is spurring the adoption of broadband at home for telecommuters, reports market researcher InStat/MDR. Some 30 million Americans spend part of their workweek in their pajamas.

Given traffic congestion and the cost of providing office space and other amenities, and given the performance-orientation of knowledge worker jobs, many enlightened companies are happy to afford their workers with this flexible workstyle. Home often is one of the best places to get real work done, and knowledge workers are likely to put in more hours, not fewer, from home.

Stat Fact

The worldwide corporate e-learning market will exceed $23 billion by 2004, representing a compound annual growth rate of 68.8 percent from 1999 through 2004, according to market research firm IDC.

In fact, increasingly companies are willing to provide the computing equipment and broadband DSL or cable-modem connections for their off-site workers. InStat has found that 40 percent of all subscribers to broadband (DSL, cable, fixed wireless and satellite) at home were subscribing for business purposes.

"The level of investment in America's remote workforce is expected to increase steadily over the coming years," says Kneko Burney, an InStat director.

That has several implications for you, the e-learning entrepreneur. First, know that business students won't always be found at their main places of business. If you pitch a company, you may need to be equipped to serve its remote workers.

On the upside, despite the relatively low penetration of broadband into homes at the moment, you can expect that infrastructure to be upgraded relatively quickly over the next couple of years. Some workers will be able to take advantage of high-bandwidth technologies such as streaming media and various kinds of audioconferencing and videoconferencing. But you'll also need a strategy to serve those for whom delivering streaming video over a dial-up connection yields poor results—a postage-stamp-size window in which the video stream is jerky and fuzzy. We'll be in a transition period that will represent a challenge for some, an opportunity for the innovative.

Stat Fact
About 19 million of the 69 million American households with Internet access have a broadband connection (cable modem, DSL, or satellite) that lets them hook up at 500 kbps or more, according to Forrester Research. The rest typically connect over 56 kbps dial-up modems.

Continuing Education: Now More than Ever

While companies were offering incredible perks to attract employees during the late 1990s, a contraction in employment levels has made the workplace more competitive than ever. In addition to millions of layoffs, record numbers of workers in their 50s, 60s, and 70s are staying in the workforce, reports outplacement firm Challenger, Gray, & Christmas. Many report that they just like what they do and would miss those with whom they work. But more say that they need the money. That forces companies to alter plans for hiring and promoting younger workers.

As it takes longer for the unemployed to get employed, they are highly motivated to upgrade their skill sets. And while the job squeeze gives employers an opportunity to raise their standards and find better-qualified workers, it's still cheaper to update someone's skills than to go through the expense, disruption, and learning curve that accompanies the hiring process. Additionally, employers still fight over certain categories of hard-to-replace workers who tend to be highly educated and in technical positions. Surveys show these workers have a distinct preference for working partly from home and communicating with the office over the Internet. It's only logical that they also would be disposed to learn over the Internet.

Looking Out for the Bottom Line

One of the biggest trends in U.S. business during the past two decades is outsourced services. Sloughing off millions of employees, the Fortune 1000 still needed to handle the same workloads. This provided a jump-start for many newly unemployed entrepreneurs, whose firms began doing basically the same tasks for their former employers.

Large corporations are still frantically looking for ways to slim down by outsourcing many tasks, says Challenger, Gray, & Christmas. Those are usually jobs not central to core revenue-generating operations. This trend will continue through good times and bad as companies strive to continuously reduce costs.

> **Beware!**
> You'll market to senior staff, but you won't have the account long if students don't report back their enthusiastic approval and management doesn't see improvement in their skills.

Outsourcing just makes economic sense. In most cases, whatever a full-time employee earns, their employer has to pay another 40 percent or so of that salary in health benefits, insurance, retirement, and other expenses. That doesn't include general and administrative costs such as office space, desks, computers, heat, light, and supplies, all of which can be substantial. A very large portion of the software development industry is composed of contract employees who may still have a desk at, and spend all their time at, a single firm. Companies of all sizes and markets are also turning more to temporary or part-time employees, who are easier to lay off and don't get the full benefits package.

And yes, companies are anxious to outsource employee training. While highly necessary, it is typically viewed as a cost center and one that external firms can handle very effectively.

What Knowledge Workers Need to Know

What do knowledge workers need to know? The short answer is "everything." Training opportunities run the gamut from building better spreadsheets to meeting regulatory guidelines to management skills. Likewise, companies increasingly want help designing and implementing courses that are unique to their firms, whether it has to do with products or processes.

Naturally, courses in the whole panoply of computer skills are central to knowledge workers. A familiarity with popular applications such as Microsoft Word, Excel, and PowerPoint is basically a prerequisite today for filling any job with opportunity for advancement. More advanced courses in project management and databases from Microsoft Access to Oracle also are very popular.

> **Smart Tip** _Tip..._
> Think about professional niches for corporate workers. For instance, RedVector.com focuses on the building and design trades. Offering more than 1,000 online courses, it works closely with businesses and universities to ensure that all courses are approved or registered with state boards and professional organizations.

Popular productivity applications also act as the front ends for more sophisticated programs and processes. Knowing them helps in managing more advanced activities like deploying and using marketing databases or supply-chain management systems.

Since all this software keeps evolving, none of us ever graduates from computer college. E-learning entrepreneurs can consider courses on computer topics as perennial moneymakers.

Data-Driven Professionals

"Collaboration" is one of the biggest buzzwords in business today. And when management types talk about collaboration, they mean at a distance.

U.S. businesses now send more than three trillion e-mail messages a year, according to international market researcher IDC. The average knowledge worker is juggling anywhere from 30 to 100 e-mails a day—not all of them welcome, of course.

Similarly startling is the speed at which new communication technology is adopted. First developed as a chat tool for computer enthusiasts just a few years ago, instant messaging (IM) has invaded the workplace in a big way. IM is growing even faster than e-mail—fast enough, in fact, to make any measure of its use obsolete before its study is complete. Web traffic researcher comScore Media Metrix estimates that people are spending something way north of 113 billion minutes a month chatting back and forth over IM. That means the average IMer is spending something like 45 minutes a day communicating. The topic of conversation is increasingly work-related.

Accounting firm Deloitte & Touche notes that we live in an age when more than half of all business documents are never printed and "e-mail has replaced the facsimile." The world took 300,000 years to produce the 12 exabytes of electronic data estimated to be in existence worldwide, reports Deloitte & Touche. (An exabyte is more than one million terabytes. What's a terabyte? A thousand gigabytes.) But this huge base of data is expected to double in two years!

Virtually overnight, workplaces have been transformed into electronic information warehouses, and the Internet and messaging have become unavoidable aspects of every knowledge worker's daily grind.

Among the implications for e-learning, a growing number of people are interested in learning how to do things that might have been considered restricted to professionals, such as Web page design. And many more need to understand Internet structure, Web design, e-commerce, and collaboration tools for their jobs.

They also may need specific information about systems such as CRM (customer resource management) and ERP (electronic resource

Dollar Stretcher
With small groups, try using one of the free instant messaging services to conduct ad hoc classroom discussion sessions online.

procurement) that are now reached through the Web. Many of the big-name vendors that are providing the infrastructure for these activities are also dipping their big toes into e-learning—including Cisco, Hewlett-Packard, IBM, Oracle, PeopleSoft, SAP, Siebel Systems, and Sun Microsystems. James Lundy, a vice president and research director at Gartner, an IT consulting firm, points to the entry of such big fish as a signal that e-learning has become mainstream.

Train Without a Plane

Stat Fact
U.S. companies spent nearly $57 billion on employee training in 2001, a third of that with outside providers, according to *Training* magazine.

Traditionally, corporations have always viewed training as a cost center—something from which they do not derive immediate revenues. Yet they also appreciate that it's a necessary investment, and they spend huge amounts every year sending employees off to seminars on a wide range of subjects.

Training costs can be open-ended. There is the cost of the training session itself, of course, as well as travel expenses that could range from gas mileage to a local hotel to airfare, and all the attendant amenities of a company retreat. Either way, the company loses the time of an employee. (This is true even if it's a weekend event—how productive is anyone on the following Monday?)

In return, the corporation hopes that employees come back more knowledgeable and better trained. But Jack Rochester, a senior analyst with IT strategic analysis firm Delphi Group, estimates that "probably 30 percent to 70 percent of what somebody learns during a three-day seminar is forgotten or of little use to them." A typical scenario, says Rochester, is that the employee leaves for the training session excited about it and determined to get the most out of it. But when that employee gets back to work, he or she faces a deskload of work that has piled up—often with new responsibilities based on the training. The notes from the training session waste away in a drawer. Three months later, the employee can't remember anything. "There's too much of that going on," says Rochester.

In this post 9/11 world where travel has become nothing but more time-consuming and expensive, both employees and corporate managers would just as soon find alternatives to boarding an airplane. E-learning is likely to be even more attractive to small to medium-sized companies that lack the budget to send employees off site.

Mixing the Best Blend

But you still need to deliver coursework that improves upon seminars delivered by traditional providers. People need incentives for adopting new ways of doing things—the lack-of-travel incentive notwithstanding.

One way to add value is to blend synchronous and asynchronous coursework with class time. Employees can study presentations and take tests online (where they can be easily updated or otherwise customized), augmenting classroom work. That's how the business education programs work at MiraCosta Community College (www.miracosta.edu) in Oceanside, California. Leon Levy, director of business development, reports enthusiastic acceptance among local firms.

Workers can take classes on campus or learn asynchronously at their own pace through the college's Web site, but MiraCosta's Business Development program also brings classes to the workplace. In addition to the usual popular computer basics and software training courses, classes are offered to improve workplace skills—English as a Second Language, Workplace Math, and Business Communications. There also are offerings for supervisors on topics like Interpersonal Communication Skills, Team Building, Conflict Resolution, and Human Motivation. For managers, MiraCosta offers courses like Problem Solving, Superior Customer Service, and Statistical Process Control. The classes blend computer use and classroom experience as appropriate.

Making It Sing

To succeed, e-learning initiatives must more than just deliver educational materials. They must become a more strategic component of the overall business environment. A corporate customer will demand more than just a simplistic text-based course. Make sure you've covered these three bases:

1. *Add interactivity.* Plain text-based training material may be useful, but it's limited. No one likes to read at length on a computer. Students won't retain as much; they'll get bored, and there'll be resistance. Corporate students are well-equipped, so add interactive elements such as simulation, collaboration, and online testing. If you don't add value above the "old ways," you're reducing your competitiveness and limiting your profit potential.

2. *Blend learning styles and keep it personal.* You'll want to highlight personal interaction with bulletin boards, e-mail, scheduled Web chats, and (if available) videoconferencing. And often you can't do away with face-to-face contact.

3. *Focus on business issues.* Focus on solving business problems and achieving business goals that can be measured. A company wants to see explicit return on the investment in your training. Will you improve their customer support organization? Enhance their sales? Enable them to train their employees in specific tasks at a reduced cost? Knowledge alone is not sufficient reward.

"We're reaching 1,100 people at work, most of whom wouldn't have a chance to take a college class if it wasn't during work hours," says Levy. "You've got a guy or gal working as a line operator or supervisor, and the spouse works and the kids need a babysitter. Neither one has the time to go to school, but one or both need to learn computer or supervisory skills. The company brings us on site and, generally, pays for the class."

The off-campus business classes, generally known in the industry as contract education, started three years ago at MiraCosta. They account for about 15 percent of the revenue for the continuing education programs that Levy oversees. "My goal is to bring that up to about 50 percent," says Levy.

His programs must be entirely self-supporting and managed as any entrepreneurial venture. Not only does he not receive any taxpayer funds, but his operation must pay the college 8 percent of his revenues for the use of college facilities. He, in turn, contracts out most of his education classes to local e-learning entrepreneurs who operate on a revenue-sharing basis.

Explains Levy, "We need someone with both an academic background and a business background."

Custom Coursework

In addition to typical computer and management subjects, some of your potential customers want courses that are unique to them. These often go beyond the usual knowledge worker productivity applications. Many have to do with special software or equipment that the company uses, or they may be task-related. Some topics will be unique to a company, or companies may ask that it be delivered in a unique way that speaks to the company's mission.

Over the years, MiraCosta has developed a core of 50 or so classes on the most popular topics such as English as a Second Language and the standard supervisory skills. When these don't suffice, a MiraCosta representative meets with the company and assesses their needs, makes a proposal, then adjusts it to the company's wishes.

Beware!
While much of the subject matter might appear standard, companies contracting employee training aren't likely to be satisfied with canned courses. They'll usually have individual requirements that require at least some customization of popular topics.

"We aren't here to present some predigested course," says Levy. "We're here to find out what a business needs and adapt our coursework to that need. Sometimes, that means adapting off-the-shelf coursework. But, for example, over the years, we've developed a customer service course that we do differently than others."

Levy is always open to proposals for new content from e-learning entrepreneurs—if it includes new content or presentation methods, and if Levy believes it will sell.

Here's one recent successful pitch: A course to teach marketing directors how to analyze customer demographics and sales potential using geographical mapping software. Students each pay $590 for the two-day course.

"Encouraging workforce development is a priority filtering down to all of California's institutions of higher learning from the executive and legislative branches of state government," reports Levy. His counterparts in other states, who he meets at education conventions, are receiving similar encouragement toward contract education from their education establishments. "Contract education is becoming increasingly important to a lot of colleges," says Levy.

Smart Tip

Often corporations must train their customers as well as their employees. And the customers aren't always business customers—sometimes they're consumers. There's a brisk business in creating interactive elements and other e-learning tools for customer support Web sites. Best Buy goes a step further, selling e-learning courses to consumers themselves.

Likewise, corporations often find that a combination of classroom work and online instruction can provide the most effective approach to employee training. E-learning is most effective when blended with traditional classes. They mix and match to meet their needs.

6

Training the Information Professional

In this chapter, we'll examine the opportunity for providing courses to IT professionals such as programmers, network administrators and Web page designers. This training could be in asynchronous self-study courses over the Net or synchronous classes delivered via videoconferencing technologies and augmented by forums, scheduled chat rooms, and other communication methods.

Obviously, you can assume a high level of computer competence among this audience. Ditto for motivation, especially since the IT employment market has gotten very tough. Career paths clearly go up the certification ladder.

Taking the Long View

Despite the dotcom meltdown and turn-of-the-millennium recession, when we step back and look at IT jobs over a longer period of time, we see that growth is assured simply because we are becoming an ever-more computer-based economy. (In fact, telecommunications, the hardest hit sector, is exactly where the most programming, network management, and security jobs are likely to be needed over the next decade.)

And e-learning entrepreneurs may be quicker than traditional educational institutions to exploit demand.

"The single biggest obstacle that community and technical colleges face is the ability to train faculty on the software the industry is currently using," says Bruce Brooks, director of Community Affairs for Microsoft. "Typically, there is an 18- to 24-month lag time between the time new technology is introduced in the marketplace and its adoption into academia."

That's a market window likely to get wider. The technology wheel keeps turning and retraining never ends. New programming languages, new protocols, new standards, and new customer support systems are being created all the time. In a sense, the next generation of IT professionals is today's IT workers, who haven't yet learned the skills they'll need to exploit technologies not yet born.

According to the U.S. Bureau of Labor Statistics, computer-related jobs will continue to experience phenomenal growth through 2010. The industry is expected to add 664,000 software engineers and 677,000 computer support specialists and systems administrators, both nearly doubling the total from 2000. All of them, like today's high-tech workers, will require continuous training.

"The worst is over for the worldwide IT training market and the overall value of training remains," says Cushing Anderson, program director for Learning Services Research at market research firm IDC. "However, to traverse the rocky road to come, vendors must focus on linking training efforts to business results, present an image of stability and reliability, and address issues of suitability of e-learning."

> ## Smart Tip
> **Tip...**
>
> What jobs will be in demand in your corner of the e-learning market? The U.S. Bureau of Labor Statistics (www.bls.gov/opub/ooq/ooqhome.htm) details growth in 270 different IT occupations through 2010. But don't overlook sectors outside IT. For example, there's a growing need for nurses, who need an increasing amount of technical medical knowledge.

Another hot button for corporations is avoiding the large-scale software failures that have plagued so many in recent years. Avoiding these problems will require a massive amount of dollars and personnel—well-trained personnel. An insistence on higher levels of expertise will create many opportunities for e-learning entrepreneurs. It also represents a challenge to produce coursework that measures up, which hasn't always been true in the past.

Remember to keep a broad view of IT needs—most notably, corporations also need training for their technical support people. Gene Kansas, from Help Desk 2000, the certification arm of IT services firm Support Technologies (www.teamstc.com), notes that "the more that people use technology, the more problems that are going to crop up. And the more problems, the more support that's needed. As technology increases, so will the demand for educated, certified people to handle it."

A job in the call center is a definite "foot in the door," adds Melissa Doble, recruiter from recruitment agency TMP Worldwide, and this "can grow into an even more technical position."

Playing It Safe

Another IT macro trend that will be with us for a long time is the need for improved security against attacks at all levels.

Skilled programmers and other high-tech workers—network administrators, help desk, and other support staff—will be needed to man the ramparts and build or manage ever-better firewalls and intrusion detection systems. With the vast number of Distributed Denial of Service (DDOS) attacks, which flood servers with so much traffic that they begin to fail, security professionals also counsel redundant sets of servers. A company can't afford for its Web site to be down.

As such threats keep growing, demand for information security personnel seems assured. One of the fastest-growing certifications in IT is Certified Information Systems Security Professional (CISSP), the "gold standard" in cyber security credentials. It's offered by the International Information Systems Security Certification Consortium (ISC)^2. The mission of this nonprofit organization is to provide a consistent standard for credentials in 85 countries.

(ISC)^2 partners with private and public organizations to offer exam and review sessions worldwide—organizations such as the Information System Security Association (ISSA), MIS Training Institute, the University of Southern California, Deloitte & Touche, IBM, the Social Security Administration, and the State Department. In addition to coursework and exams, the CISSP credential requires four years experience in information security (or three years plus a bachelor's degree) and successful completion of the CISSP exam.

(ISC)^2 reports that the number of CISSPs is up to 15,000 worldwide and is expected to continue growing rapidly. In fact, Gartner predicts that some workers with these certifications are headed for the executive floor. By 2004, says Gartner, half the world's largest companies will have an executive whose only job is the centralized development and implementation of information security policies.

Did We Mention Certifications?

Whatever an IT pro knows, he or she must prove it with a piece of paper to get a job. Career advancement requires the right course history. So be ready to provide certificates of completion that students can use as resume builders. Those may or may not differ from the certifications product vendors provide as the result of exam completion, depending on your business relationship with those vendors and whether you just do training or testing, too.

There are literally thousands of course topics covering everything from Cisco network security to the intricacies of SQL databases to information security tricks. Many are offered by or in conjunction with product manufacturers. Others are offered by professional associations, computer resellers, or other distribution organizations, news outlets, colleges, and other traditional learning institutions And many, of course, are offered by e-learning companies.

Most certificates are offered in cooperation with product providers like Cisco, Microsoft, and Oracle. Microsoft employs two independent testing companies for its certifications, but equivalent certifications are available from others. These companies have established a very deep infrastructure of coursework, certification standards, and district staff to support networks of teaching partners who, themselves, must undergo rigorous and expensive training, be tested and certified, and demonstrate certain financial and professional qualifications.

For example, Oracle sponsors its own Oracle University and also has recognized hundreds of training organizations around the world and authorized them to deliver coursework developed through Oracle University. Similarly, Microsoft operates no less than six programs through which different kinds of training partners can become certified to themselves offer Microsoft training and certifications.

These software makers have to ensure that the support network that they are creating delivers the best and most consistent information possible and the highest level of customer service consistant with profit. As such, you'll be expected to adhere to a minimum set of

Beware!
Software vendors could turn out to be your business partners upon whom you may depend for coursework, certification standards, or referrals. But maintain your objectivity with savvy high-tech students or some of the shrapnel from bad software installations could fly your way.

Smart Tip

Tip...

Large corporate trainers report that a higher share of students in e-based courses pass certification exams than those in instructor-led classes. Self-paced learning seems to improve retention rates.

standards recognized by the manufacturer as representing mastery in different products.

To take the Microsoft Certified Trainer (MCT) program as one example, you must renew your application for it online and pay a couple hundred dollars annual fee every October. To earn or renew your MCT certification, someone in your organization must hold at least one current Microsoft certification, attend a Microsoft MCT course at a Microsoft training center, demonstrate instructional skills, and have broad technical knowledge. Depending on the program, you must deliver a certain number of courses during a one-year period to be allowed to renew your MCT status. Microsoft audits a certain percentage of trainers every year to make sure they are doing the job. In return, Microsoft grants you the necessary license, access to content, information, and marketing materials, and use of Microsoft brand identifications. Above all, Microsoft will refer students to you. Depending on your business, that could be 90 percent of your whole marketing program.

Certification always involves testing. The product vendor typically creates the tests. However, Microsoft solicits input from certain high-level training organizations. Also, if the topic is relatively new or you are unusually successful, you may be able to consult with vendors and influence the training criteria.

Don't be afraid to create your own. Among the 400 certifications offered by online test center giant Brainbench are generalized topics of its own creation that go way outside IT topics—for example, $50 tests on Advertising Industry Knowledge or Pharmaceutical Industry Knowledge.

Bright Idea

To get anywhere, IT professionals need both a college degree and a string of certifications in no particular order. Some students hop back and forth between college and training courses—often while already on the job. Why not be a one-stop shop that offers both types of education online to busy IT workers?

Brainbench has acquired such credibility that, after just four years in the industry, it can afford to offer certification exams independent of the direction of product vendors. At Brainbench, a MCSE exam is, instead, a Windows Administrator exam.

"Our tests are built purely from the application point of view without vendor biases," says Brainbench co-founder Mike Littman. "We're at a more granular level, where we're really focusing on real-world issues, as opposed to focusing too much on the products themselves."

> **Smart Tip** *Tip...*
>
> What's the IT certification competition like? Find out quickly at Find Computer Schools (www.find-computer-schools.com), an IT Web portal with a powerful database of IT certification training resources searchable by training type, topic, certification type, state, ZIP code, and numerous other parameters.

Pricing the Product

Testing aside, many online courses can run as little as two to three hours or as long as 24 hours' worth of intermittent asynchronous coursework. But the typical course is between six and eight hours. Prices are all over the map—from $30 to $400 or even $600. They generally reflect market demand and the potential economic value to come from certification in that topic. In contrast, classroom-based IT courses can run as high as $2,800 a week. And that usually doesn't count certification exams or the boot camps you might attend to practice for those exams.

It also makes a difference who is offering them and where. For example, Oracle recently offered attendees of OracleWorld a series of certification exams for $50 each. The exams normally would have cost more than $100 through Oracle University. The Association for Computing Machinery (www.acm.org) offers similar online courses for free if you are one of its 75,000 dues-paying members.

Determining pricing for your courses should start with a simple Internet search of what the competition is doing. Then comes the hard part—deciding whether you are looking for high margins or rapid market penetration, and calculating how well you can communicate your unique added value to the marketplace.

As *Certification* magazine points out, IT pros pay for all or some of their training courses a little more than half the time, with employers picking up the other tabs. "They are making a very real investment, so it is natural that with such an investment, these professionals expect more than a feel-good result from their certifications—they expect an economic return."

According to *Certification* magazine's research on certifications (both in-classroom and online), the return on the investment is easily identified. Including travel and materials as well as fees, the average certification costs $1,934. Of this total amount, $338 is spent on materials. On average, more than half (53 percent) of those certified report they got a raise within the first year of attaining their primary certification, and 37 percent rec-eived a promotion.

The average student saw more than a 10 percent salary increase within the first year of attaining the

> **Smart Tip** *Tip...*
>
> Use a Macromedia Flash presentation on your Web site to give potential students a taste of what your coursework looks like before they sign up. Be sure it looks great and works without glitches because this is a critical audience.

primary certification, which equated to a $4,477 increase in salary. Several Microsoft certifications generated raises of between 14 and 24 percent.

So, cost isn't what worries potential students most when they consider taking a certification course. Instead, they worry about the time needed to complete the course. Solve that and you are likely to attract more certification seekers and can charge them more.

What's Hot

Programmers help companies develop custom IT infrastructure or work for companies that develop hardware or software. Administrators, of course, help companies implement and maintain IT infrastructure. There have always been vibrant training markets for both types of occupations; the emphasis now may be shifting slowly toward the administration side.

Timely Topics

Here are some of today's most common online course titles.

Databases—General
- Introduction to SQL
- Data Analysis

Development Solutions
- Designing Reusable Code in C++
- Common Object Model (COM) Fundamentals II

e-Business
- e-Commerce Fundamentals
- Strategies for e-Commerce Site Implementation

IT Management
- Client/Server Fundamentals
- Nework Security and Firewalls
- CompTIA's A+ Certification

Java
- Getting Started With Java
- Programming Java-Based Servlets

Linux
- Linux Basics
- Configuring Linux Networks

Networking and Security
- Systems Security Certified Practitioner Exam Cram
- Managing Web Services Using Apache Web Server

Oracle
- Oracle8i Database Administration Certification Series
- Oracle9i Upgrade Exam Cram

Project Management
- Project Cost and Quality
- Identifying and Analyzing Project Risks

Telecommunications
- Understanding Digital Subscriber Lines
- Understanding Advanced ATM

Web Development
- Learning Programming Basics for the Web
- Using Perl Programming Concepts

Programming skills most in demand include Java, Visual Basic and Visual Studio, .NET, CompTIA A+, CCNA, and Linux. Supervisory jobs include network administration, project management, programming design, customer resource management, and a wide array of security practices.

Web developers are interested in anything that enhances usability, including design and shopping cart fulfillment strategies, and applications involved in Web page design such as Microsoft FrontPage and Adobe Photoshop. There also is a need for programmers versed in more fundamental Web programming tools like HTML and XML, JavaScript, and .NET tools. (You can soon add programmable mobile phones to this list.) And, of course, training is critical in networking products, databases, server tools, and security topics of every kind.

Don't overlook professional development and managerial courses for IT pros. If they hope for advancement, they face the same personnel, scheduling, project management, and other managerial requirements that any MBA does.

Ready, Able, and Demanding

This audience is already highly educated and quite open to suitable asynchronous learning. According to surveys by *Certification* magazine, about 65 percent of IT professionals looking for certification have earned a college degree, and 18 percent have a

Who Is the Student?

Certification Magazine says your potential student looks a lot like this:

Gender	Male (84%)
Age	33
Education	College degree (65%)
Certifications held	3.86
IT experience	8.38 years
Years at company	4.18 years
Years at job	3.1 years
Job focus	Networks (34%)
Annual salary	$55,557

graduate or professional degree. The 35 percent who are not college graduates have taken classes at technical colleges and institutes.

About half of high-tech professionals are taking a course at any given time and four-fifths plan to be enrolled in one within a year. Most collect about one new certification a year.

More than a third of technical certificants work at jobs in networking—network engineering, network management, and network administration. Almost three-quarters work primarily on the Windows platform.

Expect high-tech pros to have the latest equipment—and know how to use it. Regardless of the size of the company in which they work, they are even more likely than knowledge workers in large corporations to have access to broadband connections at work and at home. They are familiar with wireless networking and have access to wireless equipment.

They know PowerPoint, Macromedia Flash, and a wide variety of other delivery options. If you are introducing them to a new technology, you can expect them to get up to speed on it quickly.

But sloppy or hastily repurposed coursework won't cut it for these students. They live and work in a multimedia world, requiring e-learning material to be engaging, if not compelling. Gadgets? You bet they have them. They also show a high degree of inquisitiveness and specific preferences about anything technological.

It's a demanding crowd, and it's quick to turn critical. IT pros will recognize different Web elements for what they are and may even get diverted into critiquing

---

Dauntless DANTES

Don't forget the armed services. Like all government agencies, the Department of Defense runs various programs to help underwrite the cost of independent training for armed forces personnel. Security is an obvious priority for all branches of the military nowadays and one such program specifically designed to certify security professionals goes by the daunting acronym of DANTES (Defense Activity for Non-Traditional Education Support).

This program reimburses members of the Army Reserve, Army National Guard, and the Air Force Reserve for information security training courses. It acquaints them with private-sector security training practices and prepares them to locate employment if and when they enter the civilian workforce. The U.S. Department of Veterans Affairs has similar reimbursements for other members of the military.

them. If you have a media-rich Web site or media-rich courses, the components had better work and better not get in the way. These students will be in a hurry and will recognize technology that is not helpful for what it is.

Resume Builders

These much sought-after certifications tell you which software platforms and vendors are likely to have established e-learning materials or course standards. They're also likely to be the most crowded e-learning markets. Will these courses be loss leaders or cash cows for you?

Database Administrator (DBA)

- Oracle Database Administrator/Developer (DBA/DEV)
- Microsoft SQL-Microsoft Certified Database Administrator (MCDBA)
- IBM DB2 Certified Advanced Technical Expert

Internet Developer

- Prosoft Certified Internet Webmaster (CIW)
- Prosoft CIW Site Designer
- CIW Web Language and Application Developer (PHP scripts or XML pages)

Network Administrator

- Microsoft Certified Systems Engineer (MCSE)
- Microsoft Certified System Developer (MCSD)
- Cisco Certified Network Administrator (CCNA)
- Cisco Certified Network Professional (CCNP)
- Novell: Certified Network Engineer (CNE)
- Sair Linux Certified Professional (LCP)
- Red Hat Certified Engineer (RHCE)
- Sun Solaris System Administrator and Network Administrator

Security

- Certified Information Systems Security Professional (CISSP)
- Security Certified Network Professional (SCNP)
- Checkpoint Certified Security Expert (CCSE)
- Check Point Certified Security Administrator (CCSA)
- Check Point Certified Quality of Service Expert (CCQE)

7

Lifelong
e-Learning

Most of the learning you do in your life has nothing to do with a degree or a certification. E-learning is carving out an ever-larger role in your personal learning—whether it's a CD-ROM that polishes your French conversational skills or an interactive quiz on a parenting education Web site.

While personal learning is the broadest of e-learning markets, it's the hardest to define and hardly the richest—not yet, anyway. Many promising and prominent ventures have flopped, such as the edutainment software companies that melted away during the past decade, or Fathom, the Internet academic consortium that quietly folded its tent in 2003.

Over time e-learning will become as deeply embedded into our personal lives as are computers and other information appliances. Entrepreneurs like you will make this happen. In this chapter, we'll sketch out some of the opportunities, starting with a look at the different demands of customers in different age groups. Some aspects may surprise you, such as the potential interest among seniors.

Kids Are Born to It

Technology is now second nature to kids. They were born into TV households; many had a remote control in their hands by the time they could walk. And they're growing up with computers.

Online market researcher InsightExpress studies show that nine out of ten students already own or have access to a computer, and about a quarter of families are shopping for another. And children also get time on computers that are appearing in ever-greater numbers in their classrooms.

A recent study done by family marketing firm Circle 1 Network and interactive strategist SpectraCom, shows that among kids ages 4 to 18 40 percent own some kind of wireless device—cell phones, pagers, handheld computers, even laptops. As you might expect, the older the kid, the better equipped.

Wireless network bandwidth isn't where it needs to be for you to beam e-learning coursework or advertising to cell phones. But when all that comes together, this generation will be equipped to receive the message—even if their original intent was just

---

Teen Drivers

They may not be interested in what you—or their parents—want to promote, but teens are very definitely tuned in to the Internet and technology in general. In fact, when it comes to any technology purchase for the family, teens rule.

"Parents may control the checkbook, but teens wield the most influence in technology purchasing decisions in American households because they have the most interest," explains research firm InsightExpress. Teens cast the deciding vote a majority of the time in the purchase of everything from MP3 players and Internet access to cellphones, digital cameras, and even handheld computers.

to chat it up with friends. You may not have long to wait. The number-one device on the wish lists of six out of ten teens is a wireless laptop because it will let them surf the Net and help with homework.

Not surprisingly, the computers are well-connected. A recent Benchmark North America study by Forrester Research found that more than 70 million American households have Internet access, almost 20 million with broadband access, and more than 40 percent of households in both categories have kids. By 2005, says Forrester, there will be more than 80 million Internet households, almost 50 million with broadband.

> **Tip...**
>
> ## Smart Tip
>
> Think niches—and sometimes even niches within niches. Take financial skills, for example: Different versions of the Investing for Success online interactive workshops have been developed by the Investment Company Institute. One was developed with the Coalition of Black Investors-Investment Education Fund. Another bilingual one was created with the Hispanic College Fund.

So what are the opportunities for e-learning in this market? While it may seem that kids are born with Nintendo controllers in their hands, they actually have a long learning curve for mastering computers. Typically this is done with a little adult guidance and a lot of trial and error. Simple e-learning "courses" and Help systems can lend a hand.

Children can can also run well-crafted educational programs on CD-ROM such as The Learning Company's Carmen Sandiego, Reader Rabbit, and Zoombinis series. Note that creating such packages, marketing them, and finding distribution for them is extremely expensive, leading, for example, to educational software publisher Riverdeep acquiring The Learning Company and other edutainment-makers who were struggling. Many Web sites offer similar but abbreviated content, typically free material that supports other products. In both cases, your entry point may be to provide contract services to those creating this content.

CD-ROMs for learning languages also have proved reasonably popular (and effective). The biggest current opportunity, however, is probably in helping children prepare for the standardized tests on which schools increasingly focus. Parents are ready to dig deep into their pockets to make sure their offspring do well on these crucial rites of passage.

These are just a few niches. Others will open to e-learning entrepreneurs with imagination, patience, and a certain amount of funding. Most of all, you'll need a clear understanding of these customers' desires.

Adult Fare

We covered college-age adults in Chapter 4. As people move on to full-time work and/or raising a family, their educational needs and desires may change dramatically. But their quest for learning continues, and it's not all about work and credentials, either.

One example is learning about software. You'd be surprised at how many people are regularly frustrated with everyday software programs such as Microsoft Word, and how few really get the most from these tools. Many are interested in learning more, for personal as well as business use. This market stays fresh because these applications change often and are so complicated and feature-rich. It really takes a lot to learn how to take full advantage of them.

> **Smart Tip** *Tip...*
>
> Libraries are moving as fast as their limited budgets allow to embrace e-learning. Perhaps the most ambitious effort is Egypt's Alexandria Library, which is attempting to put every book in the world online, and to supplement this with virtual classrooms. You may find similar opportunities closer to home. Similarly, museums may need help with e-learning services.

There's also a wide sweep of noncredit, instructor-led continuing education courses offered by community colleges and other traditional education providers. You can learn about Renaissance painting, the history of Iraq, the proper way to write a movie script, or hundreds of other subjects. There is a nationwide pool of potential customers—if you can find compelling ways to create and market these offerings. Some may be suitable, naturally, for self-study courses offered on CD-ROM or the Net. (Your best strategy may be to create the instructor-led course, and then if interest seems high enough, repackage the material into "canned" form.)

There aren't three or four continuing education markets; there are three or four thousand, depending on how you target and serve specific audiences. Some are far from obvious—such as seniors, which we'll look at next.

Seniors Go PC

Baby boomers are getting long in the tooth. The leading edge of the generation is reaching retirement age, swelling the numbers of what already was a fast-growing population of older Americans.

Everyone is living longer as a result of better medical practices, new drugs, and healthier lifestyles. Social Security Administration demographers expect the average man who retires today to live another 16 years, the average woman more than 19. The 2000 U.S. Census found that about 12 percent of the U.S. population (35 million people) were aged 65 or older, a number that is expected to double to 70 million by 2030.

Increasingly, however, this population is still on the job. A recent survey of workers aged 45 and older by the American Association of Retired Persons showed that 80 percent expect to work past 65.

Whether or not they retire, seniors can tap computers to open up a new world of information and communications. Computers can manage their finances, expand their minds, and help them fill the hours, and stay in closer touch with friends and family—an important component in living longer, healthier, and happier lives.

It's true that this is easily the least computer-literate group in our society. The Pew Internet & American Life Project found that only 15 percent of those over age 65 have used the Internet, and, of those Americans who resolve never to go online, 81 percent are over age 50.

It's not that individual seniors haven't had some experience with computers. It's just that, as a group, they have much less familiarity with them than most segments of society. Often, that's the product of an unfortunate early experience. Still, they often suffer from shame about being behind youngsters or worry that they are too old and/or too stupid to learn these newfangled gadgets.

"It's very typical for seniors to declare that they are just not good with computers," report Devin Williams and Sarah Chapman, who formed Spry Learning Co. in Portland, Oregon, to bring computer literacy and e-learning to retirees. Spry has devised dozens of classes on everything from computer basics to managing stock portfolios that have brought thousands of seniors into computing.

Williams and Chapman note that seniors are individuals with wide variations in interests and capabilities. They have found distinct differences in the manual dexterity, vision, attention span, and mental acuity of younger seniors compared with those over 70 or so. These different physical skills and learning styles require different teaching styles.

But it's worth the effort. Chapman and Williams report that they have found very little PC use among the 46,000 senior communities that are Spry's targeted niche.

Stat Fact
Once properly introduced, 69 percent of wired seniors are on the Internet every day, compared with 56 percent of other wired Americans, according to the Pew Internet & American Life Project survey.

Use It, Don't Lose It

Computers can do seniors a world of good. A study by scientists at the Rush Alzheimer's Disease Center of Chicago's Rush-Presbyterian-St. Luke's Medical Center found that more frequent participation in mentally stimulating activities is associated with a reduced risk of Alzheimer's disease (AD). The study found that, depending on the amount of increase in cognitive activities, seniors can reduce the risk of developing AD by 33 to 47 percent.

> **Smart Tip** *Tip...*
>
> The socialization aspects of education are particularly important to seniors. For many, it's not just education; it's recreation. Both personal contact and fun loom large in senior choices for e-learning providers.

The two co-founders spent a year working in senior communities before launching Spry, doing onsite research and designing their products, which ultimately turned out to be a body of coursework and teaching methods delivered in different ways. Some courses are taught over the Net, but most are taught by the recreational and nursing staff in senior communities.

"Once seniors have overcome their fear of computers, they become very enthusiastic users," report Chapman and Williams. Searching health-related Web sites for detailed information is very popular. E-mail helps with socialization because seniors aren't as isolated from distant family and friends and chat rooms promote dialogue. Computers can also offer recreation and entertainment, particularly for seniors who aren't very mobile. The machines also promote independence; people are able to carry out business activities such as shopping or personal banking from home.

While using a computer can be a physical challenge, it also can help enhance fine motor skills and hand-eye coordination for individuals who are struggling in those areas. Alternatively, accessories such as a touch pad, trackball, or voice-control system can make a computer easier to use.

Learning new skills gives seniors a sense of accomplishment that spurs them on. The mental and physical activity of computing also has been shown to sharpen the mental acuity of seniors and promote good health overall.

"But you have to take it slow and take nothing for granted—like that seniors will know when to hit the Enter key or even what an Enter key is," says Williams. You have to create coursework or lesson plans that are incredibly literal and take things step-by-step.

Continuing Education Reborn

The community outreach program of MiraCosta College in San Diego County is a good example of the varied approaches educational institutions are taking to personal e-learning. It also highlights the possibilities for entrepreneurial involvement as circumstances and student needs dictate.

Naturally, MiraCosta offers local community members a variety of computer and computer-assisted courses in the traditional classroom setting at its campuses. Most of these are conducted in partnership with local entrepreneurs.

No topic is inappropriate for online education. Some can be distinctly avante garde. For example, MiraCosta offers a class titled "Trade Worldwide in Nine Weeks." The course in building your own import/export business is delivered during two-hour synchronous lecture and discussion segments. All software and materials are downloaded on the Net. The instructor is a local e-learning entrepreneur working under the aegis of the college. He gains a certain degree of credibility from the association as well as benefiting from marketing through the college catalog and the ads Mira-Costa runs in local newspapers. He shares revenues from the classes with the college.

Most of MiraCosta's online courses are asynchronous and completely run in a revenue-sharing arrangement with EducationToGo (www.ed2go. com), an e-learning venture that offers similar turnkey e-learning courses for colleges in all 50 states and overseas. EducationToGo has a couple of hundred online courses in its catalog and more than 150 new titles in development.

> **Stat Fact**
> The majority of colleges (84 percent) report that they operate a distance learning program, with nearly half these schools offering accredited degrees over the Internet, according to market research firm Market Data Retrieval.

MiraCosta's business development director, Leon Levy, calls his school's approach pretty typical of similar institutions around the country—that is, using a blend of e-learning and traditional education modes as the situation demands.

The college's Community Services arm is not funded through tax dollars like other areas of the college. It is an entrepreneurial venture that depends on its ability to provide the courses local students want for its funding. In fact, it must turn over 8 percent of its revenues to the college. In return, it gets the use of college facilities, a considerable benefit.

And it's not a small operation. Levy's programs have 9,000 enrollments, almost as many as the 10,000 students enrolled in the tax-supported side of the college. The result is that MiraCosta is open to partnerships that will help its bottom line.

8

Solid
Foundations
for Virtual Firms

In this chapter, some of the basics that will serve as the foundations for your new business, including your mission statement, your business name and the all-important business plan will be covered.

You'll also have a few other considerations, including how to structure your company, what accreditations you may need, and how to find a good attorney and accountant to help you with the start-up process.

Mission: Entirely Possible

Why are you going into business? What is it you propose to do? Who will be your customers? What unique value will you provide them?

These are just some of the questions to consider in writing your mission statement.

A "mission statement" is a paragraph that succinctly describes the purpose and goals of your business in such a way as to appeal to all the different audiences that your business intends to serve. Your mission statement will be included in your business plan, press releases, white papers and other sales or marketing materials. It will go on your Web site under your "About" tab. It tells all those who would invest in you, partner with you, or buy from you what your business approach is all about. It also is a touchstone that can help all the members of your company stay focused on your company's goals and operating principals.

Your mission statement must grab potential customers and communicate the most important things about doing business with you in 10 or 15 seconds. It must be easy to read and understand. It must spark instant recognition among the people who you hope to reach, although not necessarily among the world at large. It must be specific enough to communicate your business purpose, and yet flexible enough to respond to what the market tells you.

Time and again, successful entrepreneurs find that they need to shift to a related audience or a different distribution methodology. For example, while he was creating the business plan for the training reseller MySoftwareHelper, Mark Carey envisioned doing most of his business with consumers from his Web site with a minority of sales coming through corporate accounts. However, after two years in business, he has found those opportunities reversed—and drastically so.

Carey wants his mission statement to appeal to single-unit buyers as well as corporate, government, and educational institutions that might buy site licenses as a result of his sales calls. On MySoftwareHelper's Web site, here's how the business is described:

"MySoftwareHelper offers the 'best-of-breed' software training solutions from leading providers for all major software applications, professional IT certifications, and 'soft skills' in a wide variety of self-paced formats to meet individual or business needs—regardless of your budget."

Note that the mission statement spells out "individual" as well as "business" needs, although individuals currently make up a minority of MySoftwareHelper sales. Note also that it specifically mentions the broad categories of courses—major software applications, professional IT certifications, and "soft skills." But it doesn't mention the vendors from whom MySoftwareHelper gets the courses, which could change. Likewise, it doesn't mention specific content like Microsoft Excel or Microsoft MCSE Certification, which are popular now, but which could later be overshadowed by newer courses.

Make Your Case to the Right Jury

Generally, a mission statement isn't meant to provide product or service specifics—it's too short. Rather, it lays out broad principals that guide the business—a commitment that should make people trust you and want to do business with you. Note the differences in the audience targeted by Spry Learning and what is being communicated in the mission statement:

"Spry Learning is dedicated to enriching the lives of older adults through life-long learning. Leveraging technology and the Internet, we seek to engage the minds and spirits of our students—keeping them healthy and connected to their families and the world. All programs are designed to benefit older adults, their residential communities and their families. Exemplary customer service is our only acceptable standard."

Again, there's nothing about the specific courses or training methodologies, even though its training methodology happens to be a key advantage for Spry. Instead, Spry outlines broad lifestyle rewards that will accrue to its customers as a result of its services. At the same time, it is unusually specific about the audience, which may well be appropriate in this case. Experience has taught the co-owners of Spry that this particular audience needs to hear this level of focus and arm-around-the-shoulder commitment.

Although both mission statements are about e-learning and both are well-directed at their target audiences, imagine if Spry tried to market to a corporate or even IT audience using that mission statement. MySoftwareHelper's mission statement probably wouldn't strike a responsive chord with seniors either. Its corporate buzzwords immediately engage businesspeople, but might be gibberish to most seniors.

Of course, these companies could easily change their mission statements on their Web sites in a few minutes, and even their written materials in a short time. But it would take a long time to change the impression of their brand that both companies have worked so hard to build and might cause confusion among customers.

Here's one more mission statement example: "Our vision is to become the leading Internet resource for continuing education, information, and communication, the essential tools our clients need to be successful in the business world."

Who's the audience here? It's different than either Spry or MySoftwareHelper, isn't it?

This is the mission statement for the e-learning Web site of RedVector.com, which provides training to people who want to get ahead in corporations and institutions. It's aimed at individuals rather than companies, as its rather uncorporate name suggests.

Start Your Own e-learning Business

Name That Firm

Picking the right name is just as important as writing an appropriate mission statement. In fact, your corporate name may even be more important since it's the first impression you will make.

Even more quickly and more succinctly than your mission statement, your business name can communicate who you are, who you serve, and even something critical about your mission. It may be very literal. It may be very subtle.

For example, RedVector.com doesn't sell to the same corporate and institutional employees MySoftwareHelper does. Rather, it's much more

Smart Tip

Tip...

What's the first question to ask if your brainstorming yields a name or URL you want to use for your business? Is it already in use? There are lots of ways to find out, but any Web search engine will give you a quick list of all the variations on your preferred name. Keep a list as you go to avoid duplication. Your search may even spark ideas for variations.

Truly Excellent e-Names

As important as it is for you to lasso a good company name, you also need a memorable Web address. These two should not diverge very much from one another.

The length and configuration of your URL, the name people type into their Web browsers to get to your Web page, can make all the difference in how many people go to the trouble of typing your name—and, therefore, navigating, to your Web site. Forget about URLs with lots of symbols and hyphens (even if they're part of your business name like "E*Trade") or complex sentences like www.creative strategiesincorporated.com. People will forget them, misspell them or just not want to do the typing, depending on how elaborate they are. For that reason, you'll want to register your own domain, as opposed to being a subset of some Internet Service Provider's domain.

You'll register for at least one domain name with one of the registration agencies—a trivial process that involves an annual fee of less than $50 (unless, of course, you are bidding on someone else's name). If your company's name is "E-learning Central," and your URL is www.elearningcentral.com, it will be relatively easy for people think of you and to get to your Web site. You'll pop up in more search engines too. But sorry, E-learning Central is one of those simple and descriptive names that are already taken. For more on setting up your company Web site, see Chapter 9 in *Start-Up Basics*.

Namestorming Worksheet

Don't have the money to pay a creative agency to think up a name for your new e-learning company? Your business name may come to you in a flash in the shower or on the freeway—or you could "brainstorm" it.

Get creative yourself by writing down as many descriptive words as you can think of that relate to your business. Here are a few to start with:

Education, training, learning, skills, development, _____

_____

_____

_____

_____

_____

Then, add other words that may relate to your target audience, such as:

Professional, career, children, seniors, IT, college,_____

_____

_____

_____

_____

_____

_____

Still others may relate to the type of training you're planning on delivering:

Programming, Web design, computer basics, networking, _____

_____

_____

_____

_____

_____

Go to an online or written thesaurus and add all the synonyms, homonyms, and, maybe, even antonyms for these words. Try some creative misspellings. Check the phone book for some ideas. If you're delivering computer-related courses, you can put an "e" in front of just about any word and come up with something different.

One way to narrow down the finalists is to write each word on a slip of paper, mix them all up, and put them together at random like Scrabble until you come up with a combination that appeals to you.

narrowly targeted to serve "professionals in the engineering, architectural, interior design, landscape architecture, building inspection, construction, and land surveying industries." This is a subset of the audience MySoftware-Helper targets—one sufficiently distinct that the two groups of customers probably overlap very little.

What does MySoftwareHelper connote compared to RedVector.com? The first sounds friendly and paternal. The second is MTV-like, assertive and cutting-edge as befits the audience of young professionals RedVector.com targets. "Vector," of course, is an engineering term. "Red" is hot and flashy, like that portion of an automobile tachometer indicating limit-pushing speeds—perhaps, like the trajectory of your career.

Spry Learning also is a good name choice for its audience. It includes "learning," which immediately tells us that it's an educational company. "Spry" might apply to a lot of audiences, but it matches perfectly with an image of active seniors.

Creative agencies charge corporations millions of dollars and take months or years to come up with the right name. In many cases, these are almost-words, collections of sounds that may be part-English, part-French, part scientific terminology. They often sound familiar, but don't have a literal meaning—at least, not at creation. What's a "Verizon"? What's a "Celica"? If you're a usual start-up, you don't have time or money to play this game seriously.

> ## Dollar Stretcher
>
> You can get an idea whether your favorite name infringes upon someone else's trademarks at NameProtect (www.nameprotect.com). It provides a partial list of trademarks using a particular word in the United States and Canada and on the Web for free, or a comprehensive list in a report for a fee. NameProtect will help you register a trademark for a fee.

> ## Smart Tip
>
> To stake out your cyber-turf, you must register not just your domain name, but also common variations of that name. You may even want to register close misspellings of the name. The popular Web search engine Google.com didn't, and now the small English town of Goole uses "Goole.com" to market local butchers, bakers, and cabinet-makers.

Brand Exercises

Your business name is a key asset, and companies frequently sue other companies, successfully, over the use of words.

That's true even for everyday words like "windows" that become part of a recognizable trademark. It's also true for slang or shorthand. For instance, even though the military has used the term "intel" as shorthand for intelligence for decades, you would be ill-advised to try to open, say, a private detective Web site which contains the word "intel" in the address. A lawsuit is almost guaranteed. Of course, you might prevail in court, but only if you have sufficient funds to prosecute your right to use the word. Even if you do, that time and effort is better placed elsewhere.

To avoid a lawsuit, your business name and product and service names must be entirely original, while sparking instant recognition. Since the word "e-learning" and most of its education-related synonyms are well-traveled, that can be a challenge. You want to be careful not to infringe upon anyone else's copyrights or trademarks.

Lawyers and Tigers and Bears

As you pick your company name, product names, and Web domain name, and as you decide the organizational structure of your company, you're probably going to need legal services. That doesn't have to be as scary and expensive as it sounds. It's not an open-ended commitment. Most of your legal bills should come as a result of issues that need to be decided before you open your doors.

Whether you operate out of a home office or downtown digs, there are several critical issues you face, subtle legal twists and turns that are beyond the experience of the layman and don't necessarily lend themselves to common sense. Unless you've been there before, you'll need a lawyer to explain the ins and outs of different methods of incorporation, copyrights, trademarks, logos, and common business contracts. Typically this should not cost more than around $1,500, but your needs may vary.

A lawyer should check to make sure that your company and product names don't infringe on anyone's copyrights or trademarks. You may want to trademark your company name and logo. You may even have a process for which you want to apply for a patent. Web businesses need a carefully crafted privacy statement and may have state tax issues. You may want to have an attorney review your Web site before it goes live.

But the most common service a lawyer will provide is helping you settle on the type of legal entity your business should be.

Many e-learning businesses operate as sole proprietorships. They're often known as Schedule C businesses because they use those forms when reporting their federal taxes. If more than one owner is involved, you may need to investigate one of several forms of

Dollar Stretcher

Don't necessarily hire the first lawyer you find—or the most expensive. Shop around, interviewing a few lawyers over the phone first and then in person. Don't be intimidated into paying hourly rates for those interviews. Also, don't hire a lawyer on a contingency basis. Insist on piecework and an estimate in advance for the cost of the specific services you need.

Bright Idea

Want to know more about incorporating? Business Filings (www.bizfilings.com) details the ins and outs for you, with a checklist of questions to ask your lawyer and price points for comparison with local legal services. For a few hundred dollars, Business Filings will even do the paperwork for you.

partnerships. In either case, if you anticipate annual revenues over $100,000, you should give serious consideration to incorporating as either a limited liability company (LLC) or an S corporation.

The principal organizational differences between the two relate to the somewhat more favorable and simpler way LLCs report taxes, while an S corp has the ability to offer stock and set up Employee Stock Option Plans (ESOPs), which help in hiring employees. Just about everything about an S corp requires a good deal more regulatory paperwork. LLCs are easier for the one- or two-person company to keep up. LLCs are probably an especially good idea as partnership vehicles since they offer more flexibility in parceling out ownership and participation of principals than some alternatives.

Any type of incorporation creates a fictitious entity—a DBA (doing business as)—that provides arms-length protection from a business lawsuit, even a frivolous one. If you are a sole proprietor, losing a lawsuit or even participating in one could mean losing your house. As a corporation, you can only lose the company under most circumstances.

A lawyer also can help you navigate local license and regulatory requirements, and write and review your contracts. (In e-learning, issues of content ownership can get tricky.) You're bound to incur some minor expense for business and tax permits—how minor will depend on your municipality and state. If you need any special permits or licenses, a lawyer can tell you.

On the bean-counting side, you may well have to collect sales tax and file the quarterly paperwork involved in that. You may also have a payroll. After working out the initial setup, these functions are carried forward by your accountant. You can easily contract with a payroll service for about $100 a month or so and have them make all the necessary deductions. As for quarterly taxes to different entities and your year-end tax obligations, these activities may involve an hour or two worth of your accountant's time per quarter and a little more at year-end.

For a more in-depth examination of the mechanics of setting up a business structure, consult Chapter 2 in *Start-Up Basics*.

Smart Tip

Keep your business taxes current. No one else—not the most aggressive credit card lender—levies interest on overdue accounts as quickly as Uncle Sam. And no one else has as good a chance of collecting. Even if you're as a limited liability corporation and go bankrupt, the IRS, and state tax authorities can hold you personally liable for these taxes plus penalties, forever.

Create a Full-Powered Plan

While you brainstorm your business name and mission statement, you should start to flesh out the details of your business plan.

This is a living document that you revise frequently as your knowledge of your market, opportunities, and abilities grow. Revising is good, especially in the early days. It's a sign of healthy growth in your understanding. Also, it may be tough to get a handle on many of the plan elements at first—particularly the forward-looking income statement. Don't worry. You'll get better at it as you go.

The business plan serves two principal purposes. First, it gives you a document that you can show potential investors and partners that encapsulates your venture and its prospects. Second, it's a blueprint or touchstone for you to use in the organization and running of your company. As your company changes, your business plan and mission statement should change with it to more accurately reflect your market opportunities.

Although it is a somewhat complicated document, you don't need to have previous experience writing a business plan. For an inexpensive jump-start, try one of several plan-writing programs such as Business Resource Software's Business Plan Write (www.brs-inc.com) or Palo Alto Software's Business Plan Pro (www.paloalto.com). Basic versions sell for $100 to $150 and are much easier to revise and much more cohesive than patching together the necessary spreadsheets and word processing documents. These packages offer templates into which you can pour your own words and numbers. They are designed by experts in marketing, planning, and strategy. Most automatically generate the proposal letters, budgets, financial charts, and other documents you'll need.

For a more detailed discussion, refer to Chapter 3 in *Start-Up Basics*. But here's a quick list of the major elements any business plan should contain:

- *Executive summary*. This is where you encapsulate your entire plan into one page compelling enough to get people to read the rest of the plan.

- *The company*. Give a brief synopsis of your company's history and goals, and include your one-paragraph mission statement.

- *Problem/solution*. What is the market need you're trying to satisfy? What's unique about your solution?

- *Market*. Describe your target market in as much detail as possible and try to quantify its growth potential.

- *Competition*. Describe who else is in the market, how successful they are, and how they differ from you. Be honest!

- *Marketing/sales*. List any current customers, and describe how you will expand that list.

- *Financial statements.* Provide a three-to-five-year forecast of revenues and expenses. Work hard on this one—it can be an eye-opener for everyone, including yourself.

- *Biographies.* This may be your strongest drawing card. Describe the backgrounds of your key executives and their unique qualifications to accomplish your company goals.

> **Smart Tip**
>
> Check out *Entrepreneur* magazine's University (www.smallbizbooks.com) for online courses that are chock-full of information about starting and running a small business.

Be Sure to Insure

You need business insurance, if only for the simple fact that nowhere is American ingenuity more amply demonstrated than in the legal profession.

Dealing with the public is fraught with liability potential. Figure on buying a million dollars worth of business liability insurance for an annual premium of around $1,500, depending on the provider. The amount has as much to do with the way they price insurance as with how much you might need—there's a relatively high initial buy-in. You can buy less, but you'll only save a few dollars a year, so you may as well have the peace of mind. Some of your business partners may require that you carry even more business insurance.

You'll need health insurance for yourself and a health plan with workers' compensation insurance if you have employees. You'll also want fire insurance for your office or home office. If you work in a flood plain or on the side of a volcano, or on the side of any mountain, you may need additional riders. Chapter 9 in *Start-Up Basics* has a lot more on insurance of all kinds as well as tips on shopping for insurance agents.

Where Credit's Due

If you're offering your e-learning customers academic credits or certifications, they need to know you are the real deal, so you must offer suitable accreditation.

No matter how great your courses are, how skilled your instructors may be, how professional looking your Web site, or even how successful you are in getting your students jobs, the world is looking for parchment, paper, a diploma, a certificate, or another sign of legitimacy.

If you're operating an online university, this is particularly important and could take awhile to achieve. Most traditional colleges and universities are accredited by one of a handful of formal accreditation bodies, and most online universities are similarly accredited.

Granted, not every institution, online or not, is accredited, and there is no legal requirement that accreditation be obtained. Many colleges operate for quite some time before achieving accreditation. But a degree from an unaccredited institution may be worthless in the job market, and it may even seem downright fraudulent to some. After all, anybody can open a business, get a fictitious business name statement,, and call themselves a university. And anyone can create his or her own accrediting organization. The Council for Higher Education Accreditation (www.chea.org) keeps watch on such organizations.

Different forms of higher education often require different forms of accreditation, and even if you're an online business taking in students from all over the world, you're subject to the laws of the district where you are physically running your business. Every state seems to take a different tack. Each has an agency that oversees higher education, which you can find in the government pages of your phone book. In Indiana, for example, it's the "Indiana Commission for Higher Education." In California, it's the "California Postsecondary Education Commission." These and similar agencies would be the best place to start learning about what procedures you have to go through to operate in your state and become accredited.

> A degree from an unaccredited institution may be worthless in the job market

At the highest level, six regional associations handle college accreditation:

1. *Middle States Association of Colleges and Schools (www.msache.org):* for Delaware, District of Columbia, Maryland, New Jersey, New York, Pennsylvania, Puerto Rico, and the Virgin Islands

2. *New England Association of Schools and Colleges (www.neasc.org):* for Connecticut, Maine, Massachusetts, New Hampshire, Rhode Island, and Vermont

3. *North Central Association of Colleges and Schools (www.ncacihe.org):* for Arizona, Arkansas, Colorado, Illinois, Indiana, Iowa, Kansas, Michigan, Minnesota, Missouri, Nebraska, New Mexico, North Dakota, Ohio, Oklahoma, South Dakota, West Virginia, Wisconsin, and Wyoming

4. *Northwest Association of Schools and Colleges (www.cocnasc.org):* for Alaska, Idaho, Montana, Nevada, Oregon, Utah, and Washington

5. *Southern Association of Colleges and Schools (www.sacs.org):* for Alabama, Florida, Georgia, Kentucky, Louisiana, Mississippi, North Carolina, South Carolina, Tennessee, Texas, and Virginia

6. *Western Association of Schools and Colleges (www.wascweb.org):* for American Samoa, California, Hawaii, and Guam

Some schools are also accredited by professional accrediting agencies. For example, law schools are accredited by the American Bar Association, and medical schools by the

American Medical Association or the Association of American Medical Colleges. Computer Science schools may be accredited by the Computing Sciences Accreditation Board (www.csab.org), and engineering schools by the Accrediting Board for Engineering and Technology (www.abet.org).

The story is different outside academia. If you're providing courses that lead up to students taking the MCSE, you may need only accreditation from Microsoft or other vendors whose products are the topic of the courses.

9

Putting Your
Money Down

In this chapter, we'll discuss some typical start-up costs you can expect when setting up various types of e-learning businesses.

We'll also discuss the pros and cons of having a homebased business vs. working out of commercial office space. We'll take a look at how some of the entrepreneurs we interviewed got their start in business and offer some tips for saving money.

This is budgeting basics. If you've already run a company or gotten money out of a venture capitalist, you can probably skim this chapter since you've either done this before or have people working for you with that experience.

Penny Pinching

There are many different ways to go into the e-learning business. Each has its own infrastructure and expense requirements.

And different entrepreneurs do the same thing in different ways. Are you someone disciplined enough to operate from a home office, or are there so many distractions in your household that you need to leave for an office every morning? Are you dipping a toe in the water with an informational Web portal or are you going full bore with an online university or highly transactional Web site complete with shopping cart?

The growth component in your five-year plan is a factor, too. Many e-learning companies start very modestly and then grow very rapidly—that is, those that survive.

There's no standard cookie-cutter list of start-up expenses. Instead, we'll give an overview of common scenarios and the expenses involved, and provide some planning tools.

As always, money is the driving factor. We assume you want to get the ball rolling spending as little as possible. If you aren't concerned about your start-up capital, you should be. No matter how much you have, there will be unbudgeted surprises around nearly every corner, and cash flow isn't likely to start flowing as soon as you think it will. (And remember that you've got your own living expenses in the meantime.)

Successful entrepreneurs emphasize that fiscal discipline fosters a kind of ingenuity and operating discipline that puts them in good standing when those inevitable challenges arise. Financial problem-solving is a boot camp of sorts for training the mind in creative sales and marketing solutions.

"For an object lesson in what happens when cash-rich companies pursue the opposite strategy, just look at the first wave of dotcoms," notes Ed Harris, co-founder of Precision Information, a personal financial education firm. SuperBowl TV ads, fancy office space and corporate perks didn't help at all when these

> **Smart Tip** *Tip...*
>
> Purchase computer and other office equipment in dollar amounts that will allow you to expense the total on your tax return, rather than depreciating it. The precise dollar amount will vary with your projected tax obligations for a given year; consult your accountant. But expensing equipment saves paperwork and almost always provides more tax advantage than depreciating it.

Dollar Stretcher

Don't lease office space—sublet. The commercial real estate market swings between scarcity and glut fairly rapidly. Even in times of scarcity, companies with long-term leases overestimate their space needs or suffer reversals of fortune. Search out distress cases in the classified ad sections of local newspapers, advertisers, or professional journals. But make sure that subleasing is allowed on the original lease.

companies couldn't convert page clicks, viral marketing, and other New Economy revenue models into receivables.

"Having money isn't the only answer to the business challenges you'll face," says Harris, who has been involved in six start-up ventures, including Persoft, one of the nation's most successful software companies, in the late 1980s. "With Persoft, we were all totally inexperienced. But we were fortunate—and I mean fortunate—that we didn't have any money at all, so we could bootstrap slowly and learned the discipline of running the business lean. These are skills people just don't learn if they have a lot of money in the bank."

Harris recalls a cross-town competitor with great technology and enough venture capital funding that it didn't need to develop those management skills. It lasted a year, while Harris' company, profitable in its first year and every year thereafter, survived to grow to $22 million in annual revenues before Harris sold it. Harris sought, then turned down, venture capital money when the venture capitalists insisted on giving him twice what he needed on the condition he grow twice as fast as he wanted.

So even if you've just landed a big chunk of VC cash—or more likely an option on a big chunk of VC cash—try to spend as little as possible. Remember, you can't reach into someone else's wallet without giving up some control of your company.

Innovate, invent your own approaches, and never take the first price offered you for anything, says Mark Carey, founder of training software reseller MySoftwareHelper. Carey never pays "list" for anything—not a car, a lawyer, or a box of office supplies at Costco. He shops around and uses the price he gets from one supplier to negotiate with another.

"It's absolutely amazing what people will do to get your business," he says. "But if you don't ask, you'll pay full sticker price or worse."

Down Home or Downtown

Precision Information has brought financial education to a million individuals and partnered with some of the largest software and financial services companies in the country. Its four equity partners work out of a modest office—an office that doesn't see the partners very often.

LearnKey, one of the largest nationwide providers of e-learning content, started in its owner's basement. Most of the resellers who now sell LearnKey's courseware to corporations, and sometimes sell a hundred or thousand copies or licenses of the courseware at a time, are still one or two individuals operating from home.

Most e-learning opportunities can be germinated in a home office. But some ventures will require a dedicated location. Mark Carey worked as a sales representative and consultant from a home office for two decades. But when he started MySoftwareHelper, he knew that he needed a small office both because broadband Internet service wasn't available in his rural Washington hometown and because he knew he would need to hire a couple of critical employees early on. (One was hired for technical expertise, the other for experience selling into the education and government markets.)

>
>
> **Dollar Stretcher**
>
> How many cell phones do you need for you and your staff? One way to find out is to buy—not subscribe to—Hop-On (www.hop-on.com) mobile phones. These are being launched in retailers and convenience stores. For $40, you get 60 minutes of service on a disposable phone. Additional talk time is available in 60-, 90- and 120-minute increments.

As we go deeper into the age of communications, the traditional constraints of time and space become less so. Even the largest clients are comfortable doing business with operations whose corporate headquarters is a basement, back bedroom, or even kitchen table. Usually, they never know. One approach is to set up a small office close to home. Spry Learning is doing $4 million annually and operating a nationwide training network that reaches thousands of seniors from a small office in downtown Portland.

The price of office space and utilities will, of course, vary widely with your community. Flexibility of lease terms will vary with the availability of office space in your town. If you have a space that permits you to work from home, you obviously have reduced your start-up costs to a small amount for office equipment and a small delta above your current living expenses. While commercial real estate may be cheap in North Sioux City, South Dakota (where Gateway Computer started), even the tiniest commercial space in San Francisco can be a burden.

But there are always deals to be had if you hunt for them, especially in a real estate downturn. You'll be surprised what you can find with a little ingenuity. Mark Carey found extremely nice digs in a lawyer's office in downtown Tacoma, Washington, by looking for a firm in a bind. As luck would have it, he found a law firm with too many offices on its hands and a five-year lease. He got a two-room office with all the amenities, including a large communal conference room, with all utilities paid for $400 a month.

We'll look in detail first at setting up a simple, one-person home office, and then a more ambitious commercial office, with multiple employees.

Home Base

Much has been written about how to actually set up a home office; simply search through the Entrepreneur.com Web site for plenty of advice. One key is to carve out a dedicated space in your home. That minimizes interruptions and lets you mentally shift from home life to work life.

Naturally, you will need the usual array of office equipment—phone, personal computer, printer, scanner, copier, fax, desk, and filing cabinet. You may choose to buy a printer, scanner, and copier separately or you might buy a multifunction device. There are pros and cons to each: a multifunction device is probably cheaper and saves space, but you'll probably give up some flexibility in choosing the features you want. Also, rather than a stand-alone fax machine, you may be able to get by on the fax board in most PCs.

Homebased Start-Up Expenses

First-Year Home-Office Expenses	Estimate	Actual
Phone lines (2 landlines, 1 cell phone)	$3,000	
Utilities (above and beyond home use)	400	
High-speed Internet access	600	
Basic office equipment and furniture	1,000	
1 Windows PC	1,200	
1 Windows laptop	1,800	
Laser printer, scanner, copier, fax	700	
Software (office suite, security, accounting)	1,600	
Web site design—simple site	500	
Web site hosting	250	
Insurance (fire, health, personal liability)	5,000	
Legal and accounting services (incorporation, trademark search, contract review, tax filings)	2,000	
Licenses/permits	250	
Subscriptions to trade journals	100	
Association membership dues	300	
Advertising/marketing	2,500	
Miscellaneous supplies	500	
Total Start-Up Expenses	**$21,700**	

All your hardware together shouldn't cost more than $6,000—probably less since you probably already have some of this equipment from past businesses or personal use. To be conservative, we price them separately in the worksheet on page 83.

You'll also want a dedicated business phone line, voice mail, a broadband Internet connection, and probably a second phone line that can double for fax and backup Internet access.

For software, you'll need a basic suite of business productivity applications plus any special tools for creating or delivering your wares or your Web site.

The accompanying "Homebased Start-Up Expenses" worksheet on page 83 shows a sample first-year outlay for an e-learning business run out of a home office. It also suggests some of the issues to consider in getting this type of business started.

Suite Software Success

You'll need the standard office productivity applications—word processor, spreadsheet, database, desktop presentation, e-mail, and scheduling software. Microsoft Office bundles all these applications together for between $500 and $600, depending on where and how you buy it. In some cases, you may have Office bundled with a new PC.

However, also popular and far less expensive are Corel WordPerfect Office and Lotus SmartSuite. These long-standing bundles have all the same types of programs with the same features as are in Office and will read all the files created in Microsoft Office, except functions that have been programmed in by someone using Microsoft Visual Basic. Sun's StarOffice Suite also offers solid functionality, a good level of Office compatibility, and a price tag around $40.

Even if you use an accountant, you should still track your income and outgo in your own accounting program such as Intuit's QuickBooks (www.intuit.com), which retails for around $225; or, at least, a small business-oriented personal finance manager like Quicken Home & Business which can be found for around $50, depending on the version. You'll also need to protect yourself from attack with a robust anti-virus, firewall, intrusion-detection package, such as Zone Alarm Professional from Zone Labs (www.zonelabs.com) for around $50.

And, of course, you'll need special software for creating content, building Web sites or databases, and any other tasks specific to your business.

Warning: Don't be tempted to save money by copying software programs. It's illegal, you are increasingly likely to get caught, and the financial penalties could put you out of business.

You should be able to keep your first-year legal and accounting expenses at around $2,000, depending as always on your locale. You will incur a few hundred dollars in expenses for business and tax permits. You may well have to collect sales tax and file the quarterly paperwork involved in that. That may involve an hour or two worth of accountant's time per quarter, and a few more hours for filing year-end taxes. You'll spend about $1,500 for basic legal services to set up your company, make sure you aren't infringing on anyone's patents, copyrights, or trademarks and, perhaps, trademark your company name and logo. You may also want a lawyer to look over your standard contracts and Web site.

Beware!
Be sure to keep business and personal expenses separate. Entrepreneurs who mingle business and personal cash often run into trouble with the flow of both. The easiest way to keep the two separate is with separate credit cards for business expenses, downloaded into finance or accounting software such as Quicken Home & Business or QuickBooks.

Beyond that, you must add expenses that are specific to the business you are building, such as courseware purchased from others or development costs for content you create yourself.

Your other major budget item will be marketing: advertising, public relations, and promotions. Customers don't just appear—you must go and gather them. Your best marketing approach will vary by the audience you're trying to reach, and you'll probably discover it only through trial and error.

A basic, informational Web site is a must-have. Getting it listed properly in various portals and search engines may cost you (and also think about targeted Web ads such as Google search ads, which can be quite cost-effective). You won't necessarily be selling directly from your site. The minimum is a kind of electronic business card that establishes your legitimacy and provides a wealth of information on your products and services.

Some recommend that you spend about 10 to 15 percent of your budget on marketing, although this is a somewhat arbitrary figure. Budgets vary tremendously by company. For example, Precision Information employs traditional advertising and public relations campaigns, while MySoftwareHelper's Mark Carey has found that they do very little for his corporate training business. He gets most of his leads from trade shows and from cold calls generated by leads developed from successful sales.

Picks in Commercial Space

Your start-up may be too ambitious or too logistically complex to launch in a home office; if so, start-up costs may be considerably greater. You may prefer to deliver your IT e-learning content in a physical classroom with a network of PCs, for instance. Or you may create sophisticated coursework with a team of developers. Or you may launch an online university or other initiative that requires regular office space.

> **Dollar Stretcher**
>
>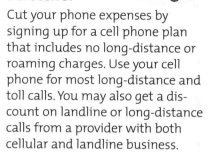
>
> Cut your phone expenses by signing up for a cell phone plan that includes no long-distance or roaming charges. Use your cell phone for most long-distance and toll calls. You may also get a discount on landline or long-distance calls from a provider with both cellular and landline business.

You'll need not only commercial space and more computer equipment or other e-learning aids but employees (either hired or contract workers).

Most of your first-year expenses will include the same budget items you would incur when setting up a homebased business. But there are some very expensive differences.

Surprisingly, office space may not be the most onerous of them, depending on how the commercial space market in your area is doing and how large a classroom you'll need. You probably won't need a lot of space to start. We use a moderately priced office of $600 a month on the accompanying "Commercial Office Start-Up Expenses" worksheet on page 87 for the typical first-year outlay for an e-learning business run out of commercial space. Change that as necessary for your locale.

You'll need a small group of networked computers. We'll add the minimum two PCs and a server setup to our budget worksheet on page 87.

Depending on what you're offering, your Web site could cost a few hundred dollars or a few hundred thousand. Such vagaries and options make it difficult to offer a cookie-cutter budget. But the worksheet is a start.

Remember to give yourself liability protection by incorporating. You may have more contracts with either higher-dollar figures or more complexity as well as thornier accounting and tax challenges than a homebased business by virtue of having employees. Again, you can find all the basics of incorporation in Chapter 2 in *Start-Up Basics*.

For marketing, we'll stick with 10 to 15 percent of your overall budget. Beyond the Web site, you may want to advertise in professional or association journals or other publications, make appearances at conferences or trade shows, or find other venues.

Don't forget memberships in professional associations such as the American Society of Training and Development (www.astd.org) or the U.S. Distance Learning Association (www.usdla.org), which offer many benefits for e-learning companies.

If utilities aren't bundled, you've got bills that will depend on your location. Heating, cooling, and lights can vary from $75 a month in the summertime to $500 during winter months in cold climates. We've estimated an annual total of $3,300. But you can get a much more precise estimate easily just by adding up a year's worth of utility bills for your home and adding, say, another 25 percent for every employee in your office. While most of your business utility expense is already accounted for in your home utility bills (with just a little extra if you have a home office), it's a separate expense if you rent commercial space.

Likewise, your first-year phone bill will depend on how much cold calling you do over what area and what kind of services you need. For starters, you'll need one voice line with voice mail and probably a fax/Internet dial-up line. You may need an 800 number if, for example, you are soliciting IT students from outside your state. Naturally, you'll also want a cell phone for yourself and, maybe, for some employees. Phone costs can vary considerably, but many communications companies have different bundling arrangements where they cut rates on your long-distance bill to get your cellular business, too—or vice versa.

Commercial Office Start-Up Expenses

First-Year Commercial Office Expenses	Estimate	Actual
Rent	$7,200	
Phone lines (2 landlines, 1 cell phone)	3,000	
Utilities	3,300	
High-speed Internet access	600	
Basic office equipment and furniture	2,500	
2 PCs, one server	3,000	
2 laptops	3,800	
Laser printer, scanner, copier, fax	700	
Software (office suite, security, accounting, networking)	3,200	
Web site design/development	25,000	
Web site hosting	1,200	
Insurance (fire, health, personal liability)	8,000	
Legal/accounting services (incorporation, trademark registration, contract review, quarterly taxes)	2,000	
Licenses/permits	250	
Subscriptions to trade journals	100	
Association membership dues	300	
Advertising/marketing	5,000	
Payroll services	1,200	
Payroll and benefits (for one employee)	40,000	
Miscellaneous supplies	500	
Total Start-Up Expenses	**$110,850**	

Beware! Delivering e-learning on the Web is no marketing panacea. One e-learning courseware provider, who anticipated annual revenues of $150,000 when it launched its highly professional, interactive Web site a couple years ago, has only been able to generate around $5,000 annually so far. As always, you must find potential customers and actually close the sale.

You should have a broadband Internet connection—with at least a DSL connection, or T1 if you're hiring more than a handful or running a public Web server yourself.

It's typically cheaper and far more effective, however, to have your Web computer infrastructure hosted by a company in that business. They can provide the necessary security, backup, and environmental controls as well as immediate scalability to keep pace with your Web site growth.

The site itself might be a very simple one, designed by you or a graphic artist friend and hosted by your ISP for as little as $10 a month plus domain-name charges. But if you'll be doing business over your Web site, your costs will be major. E-commerce sites are complex both on the front and back end. They require sophisticated databases on the back end and thoughtful and professional design elements on the front, and none of that comes cheap. Design elements and back-end programming are best left to professionals. If that's not you, put your effort into picking the right professionals.

Mark Carey of MySoftwareHelper paid $30,000 to an ad agency for creative work on his site and $19,000 to a pair of Web designers and programmers to build his site. He is convinced that he got a bargain. He shopped around for months and got estimates of up to $250,000. And the proposals often included monthly service fees. Carey insisted that his Web site designers provide easy-to-use templates so he could update his site himself.

Like any business, you'll need insurance—at least $1 million in business liability insurance for a cost of somewhere around $1,500. You can buy less, but you won't save much.

You'll also need health insurance for at least one employee—you. Figure $250 a month or $3,000 a year for an HMO plan that just covers you. As you probably are aware, health costs can be all over the map, depending on your age and locale and whether you're covering family members or setting up an employee plan. Ditto for fire, earthquake, and other insurance.

Bottom line: Except for a little more computer hardware and a fancy Web site if needed, the cost of setting up an e-learning business probably doesn't vary that much from most other sales and service-oriented concerns that require some degree of expertise. Also note that, as with any entrepreneurial venture, you may earn little or no revenue in the first months. Since your costs are greater than with a homebased business, you'll be under more pressure.

10

Content
and Delivery

In this chapter, we'll focus on two of the most critical elements of any e-learning business: content and how it is delivered.

We'll take a look at the options for developing or buying e-learning course content, as well as the various methods you can choose to deliver that content to your customers. We'll cover ways to blend e-learning with classroom work.

E-learning can cover any topic for which there's a paying customer (and that customer isn't always the student). It can be "canned" or live, as simple as text on an HTML page or as complicated as training simulations for astronauts. Content can be built with tools ranging from a word processor to a course management system to Macromedia Flash to a thousand distinctive software platforms. Delivery can be any way a computer will accept content. So don't expect a cookie-cutter guide!

Content Is King

Content is, and always has been king. But it has a troubled reign.

While there are outstanding courses being developed all the time, e-learning content still has a lot of room to improve. That spells O-P-P-O-R-T-U-N-I-T-Y for would-be content creators. It's also something of a hurdle for the sellers of e-learning services, especially among corporate or institutional customers who might have experienced inferior courseware in the past.

Course content is inextricably linked to the way it is delivered—both delivery mechanisms and that indefinable quality known as "teaching."

Delivery can be in real-time in a synchronous course led by an instructor, or at the student's convenience over a few weeks or months in a course delivered asynchronously via instructor, or totally self-directed and self-paced, or in some combination of these.

Each approach appeals in different ways. IT workers, for instance, often love the convenience of self-directed material. But that delivery mechanism is inappropriate for many other courses whose topics are not so tightly constrained, such as English 101.

Additionally, individual audience members may have distinct preferences as to how content is delivered, since people prefer to learn in different ways. Some people are readers, some are viewers, and some need a hands-on experience. One strategy for coping with that is to provide multiple delivery options.

Remember that if you are creating content with your own user interface, you need feedback on the user interface from people who are not involved in the development project. The user interface must be both easy to learn and efficient to run. Software vendors may spend thousands of dollars on usability testing. You can often get a very similar reality check by finding volunteers who represent your target market and will give you honest assessments, and paying them a small fee.

You need to take the art and science of learning very seriously. Hundreds of books have been written about e-learning. One of the very best is *Michael Allen's Guide to e-Learning* (John Wiley & Sons) by Michael W. Allen.

The wide range of subject matter and audience types to which e-learning can be delivered makes it difficult to generalize about what constitutes good content and delivery. But your customers will know it when they see it.

Getting Beyond Text

"Computer training from books doesn't work," asserts Mark Carey of MySoftwareHelper. "They are just far too wordy and make things far more complicated than they need to be. I am the kind of person who needs to have it shown to me as opposed to explained to me. Most people don't like to read."

That's not limited to computer training. The best e-learning courseware is experiential, blending highly illustrative content—video, animation, photos, or realistic diagrams—with student interactivity. That's why LearnKey, in St. George, Utah, spends so much to create videos of real instructors doing real things in its courseware.

Of course, e-learners don't necessarily have access to a classroom, or a broadband Internet connection, or even a computer every minute of every day. Books, workbooks, or videos can be useful adjuncts to courseware.

That's particularly true for IT courses. Many IT certificate-seekers appreciate having a hard-copy reference to go along with a certification course, which can take months to complete. One multi-certificate holder says that he always buys a $40 computer book to go along with his certification courses that can cost $800 to $2,000.

Bottom line: There isn't one road to learning, and the roads are not mutually exclusive. Finding the right blend of textual and visual content for a particular audience is not a trivial task. How well you solve it will have a lot to do with your success.

> **Tip...**
>
> ## Smart Tip
> Want to get an idea of just how inadequate and confusing text-based instruction can be? Click the Windows Help menu and select a topic, any topic. Note how the simplest task requires excessive explanation and steps that are made confusing by describing in words something that is meant to be seen and acted upon.

"We surveyed 700 managers in 30 different industries and asked them what they're most commonly using to create e-learning environments," says Jack Rochester of the Delphi Group, an IT business strategy firm. "Everybody's using books. Everybody's using CD-ROMs. Everybody's using videotapes. We found that the most common thing they were doing was using existing PowerPoint presentations."

That leaves plenty of room for improvement—and entrepreneurial opportunities.

Instruction Beyond Instructors

You can't divorce content from the content deliverer or from the delivery method. It doesn't matter how good the course is if the teacher or delivery method can't get it across.

E-learning courseware frees us from the constraints of time and space and provides us an opportunity to deliver high-quality instruction to a much broader audience than possible through traditional classroom training. A good instructor with good content can reach many more people than through traditional modalities.

But unlike traditional courses, good e-learning courseware doesn't just depend on the instructor—it's a team effort.

"The most important thing is not really the interactivity or the multimedia experience," says Morten Sohlberg, who runs Sessions.edu, an online Web design school in New York City. "It's the ability of an organization to pull together a very large team of people."

Creating a good e-learning course is like making a good motion picture, says Sohlberg. While classic classrooms focus on the instructor, the best e-learning methodologies bring together a group of people to create a highly specialized and creative product. The importance of the instructor is not diminished, but the talents of more specialists can be brought to bear.

Content at Sohlberg's institution comes from a combination of the instructor's knowledge and research, input from other educators, and a variety of designers and producers. "The content that you're absorbing is bound to be so much better than what one person could bring to a classroom," says Sohlberg.

Resale Value

Not every e-learning provider is as ambitious as Sohlberg and others who create their own content. You can choose from existing content and add value as you resell it.

Sometimes content can be repurposed by combining material of your own with it. You might add study guides of your own creation, components tailored for certain customers, or other elements that enhance the experience for the student. Some content publishers make this easier to do than others.

> **Tip...**
>
> **Smart Tip**
> How much should you pay a publisher for content? The discount off the retail price varies by the amount you buy and other contract conditions. In general, expect margins of 40 to 50 percent for starters.

For example, one customer for Precision Information's "Encyclopedia of Personal Finance" is a financial services consultant who uses it as a starting point to help government human resource managers explain 401(k) options to employees. Delivered via CD-ROM or server, the encyclopedia also lets employees explore other personal finance topics at their leisure. Precision Information's personal finance database is so flexible that the company can quickly produce custom courses for large financial services companies such as New York Life.

There are huge catalogs of content available on the Web from numerous providers. You might choose to resell them to institutions, use them as the basis for your syllabus in your own training center, or as the courseware for your own e-learning Web portal. In the latter case, your students are usually directed to the servers of the courseware provider's server—under your banner.

Smart Tip

If you're training IT students to pass a certification exam dealing with a particular software vendor's content, you may have to acquire course material, study guides, and manuals from that vendor or its publishing arm. For example, Cisco Press has the inside track on Cisco hardware certification specifications long before others get that information.

But if you don't want to be perceived as merely a me-too marketer of a commodity, you must add value to the courses you deliver. MySoftwareHelper aids customers by selecting the appropriate course from different publishers.

"We aren't selling a product, we're selling a solution," says Mark Carey of MySoftwareHelper, who delivers mostly LearnKey courseware to corporations, government and educational institutions. "LearnKey is an outstanding course developer," Carey says. But LearnKey doesn't have a course for every topic, so Carey fills in the gaps with a couple of other brands.

MySoftwareHelper provides needs assessment, courseware recommendations, and system integration for its high-ticket clients. They generally buy site licenses to courseware that is hosted on their own or the publisher's servers and is downloaded by employees/students at their convenience.

Neither Carey nor his account executives have a teaching background. But they can demo the products, install pilots, answer questions, and, in Carey's words, "make things happen." He has developed collateral materials to help companies successfully deploy the products and ease employees into them.

"Here is where other companies fall short—they don't understand that bringing a product in is only 10 percent of the job," says Carey. "You have to make sure it is used successfully, or they won't renew their license. If no one even knows it's available, what good have you done? But if everyone becomes familiar with a particular training modality, they won't want to use anything different."

MySoftwareHelper's company tagline is: "The Source for Software Training Solutions." Whether you aspire to be a courseware developer, a reseller or an instructor, it's not a bad philosophy to adopt. Clients won't be satisfied with just buying courseware or taking a class. Their training goals need to be satisfied.

Note that the list of e-learning resellers is much broader than you might expect, including colleges, Best Buy, Barnes and Noble and many other outlets. You may find competition in places you don't expect (or, if you create your own content, new distribution outlets).

Grow Your Own

Precision Information co-founder Joe Saari saw a need for a database in one of the oldest and most vigorously debated areas of human knowledge. Despite the reams that have been written on financial topics, there was no single source for the many, rather sophisticated, financial topics that affect every one of us. Of those sources that came close, Saari judged that none could easily be tapped.

So Saari created the "Encyclopedia of Personal Finance" to meet this need. His encyclopedia (which is really interactive courseware complete with testing) generally doesn't provide new information. Instead it rounds up time-tested financial knowledge and assembles it into one easily accessible source.

This is a more difficult, risky, and time-consuming way to build your e-learning business. You must spot a market, offer relevant expertise in the topic, and be highly skilled in all the required aspects of content creation. Professional-quality content requires you to marshal considerable resources, including individuals with expertise from numerous disciplines.

You need subject-matter experts who are the best of breed to create the material. Then you need a production arm, which can take that rough material and turn it into

---

Help Wanted (Freelance)

The world is full of freelance and wannabe writers. If you're planning on hiring one of them to work on your e-learning courseware, you'll want a writer with a proven track record—not someone just out of a school or someone who's written a handful of articles for their hometown newspaper. It's especially useful if you can find a writer who has written about the subject of your course. For example, if you plan to offer a course in network security, find someone who has published articles in the trade press on that topic. It's even better to find someone who also is familiar with teaching principals.

Additionally, the world is full of freelance graphic artists, programmers, and others with invaluable technical expertise. When possible, especially in the early days, get them under contract rather than hire them. If they work out and your business expands, go ahead and bring them on full time.

a product. The product must go through extensive quality testing for various computer platforms and scenarios. Then, of course, you need a publishing and distribution arm, which can involve many different kinds of media.

The cost of creating a course can vary with the content, production values, and the notoriety of the instructor, as well as fixed start-up costs for facilities and amortized general and administrative costs for a continuing production operation. Courses that enjoy wide distribution in the market can cost $30,000 or more to produce, says MySoftwareHelper's Carey. "It's a very expensive process, and it can take months to create a title."

You'll want to accurately access your personal strengths and weaknesses, consider opportunity costs, and be very sure of the need for your course idea. There is a vast pool of e-learning content for markets where you don't really need to reinvent the wheel. Test the waters. Look at competing products. But if you have an idea for something really special . . . .

Making the Delivery

OK, people learn via conventional classrooms, self-paced learning, instructor-led asynchronous courses, and instructor-led synchronous courses. Which is best? What's the trend?

Increasingly, e-learning is taking place using blends of these different delivery methods as the occasion demands. This is called, logically enough, blended learning. Some programs, especially full-degree programs, conduct most classes online, but still require students to gather for at least one session each term. Even if you don't have a physical classroom, you can still have a classroom session.

"In our Ph.D. program, the learners are required to attend a true residential session once a period," says Stephen Shank of Capella University (www.capellauniversity.edu) in Minneapolis. "We actually rent a college campus to do that. In addition, those same learners attend two seminars a year, which are held in hotel conference spaces around the country." Everything else is online.

Online classes do lack a classroom's level of intimacy between instructor and student and among the students themselves, with actual eye-to-eye contact, plus the immediacy of being able to get a lesson and ask a question, then ask another question based on the answer to the first question. Sometimes the answer comes from the teacher, sometimes from another student. This is ad hoc, immediate gratification for an issue that otherwise might just wash downstream.

On the flip side, online courses may let students come up with more thoughtful responses that lead to highly valuable discussions that go on for days on the course's bulletin board. People who feel awkward about speaking up in a physical classroom may come out of their shells to make important contributions.

Online learning organizations have many interactive elements that they can add to their online "schools" that make them almost like being there. Using various Web technologies (including video, if the infrastructure supports it), making live instructors available at specified hours, and promoting extensive interaction among classmates all go toward minimizing the loss of immediate personal contact.

Spohn Training (www.spohntraining.com) in Austin, Texas, exemplifies the blended approach, combining both classroom and online learning effectively in interactive synchronous classes.

"If you're trying to learn the basics of data communications such as 'what's a switch,' then CBT (computer-based training) or e-learning can be somewhat effective," says

---

Multimedia Made Easy

LearnKey (www.learnkey.com) offers an e-learning solution known as OnlineExpert, which prepares students for certifications from Cisco, CompTIA, and Microsoft. The company combines text and streaming media, presenting students with an array of industry-related articles to read along with an interactive tutorial. The tutorial involves a videotaped expert with high-production values created at considerable expense. It also includes a white board and a subset of the application itself.

Students must have RealPlayer, a utility from Real Networks that delivers streaming media. The basic version of RealPlayer is available free, although content providers must purchase the content-creation version.

LearnKey can deliver this even over a dial-up line by sending the student a CD-ROM that includes the compressed content of a course, which originally occupied a half-dozen CDs. LearnKey's MediaPoint technology unlocks and decompresses it by sending commands over the phone line from its OnlineExpert Web site. Students also get a chance for a little personal interaction by participating in LearnKey forums. You can jump ahead or jump back as you please.

You take a pretest and a post-test. The pretest covers basic knowledge, and gives students a chance to see what they know before they get into the meat of the tutorial. The pretest is a great way to ease into the subject matter, and give students a little confidence by offering some simple questions with easy answers. The post-test, of course, is a little harder and covers the material presented in the tutorial. It isn't the certification test itself, but if you can pass the post-test, you can probably pass the official certification test.

Pricing is appropriate to value. Students pay $795 for the A+ Certification bundle, for example, which includes eight sessions, a master exam, study guide, and e-support.

founder Darren Spohn. "But the more complex the training you get, the less you can do via e-learning."

Global Knowledge (www.globalknowledge.com) in Cary, North Carolina, is another instance of a company offering instructor-led e-learning. The organization, which has classrooms throughout the world, takes selected existing instructor-led courses and repurposes them for instructor-led e-learning, using two-way voice-over-Internet services. The classes are specifically designed to be an Internet class; you're not looking into a live classroom. The company uses client software plus a headset and microphone to allow each student to participate in real time. The software provides a voice connection and a shared whiteboard, and the ability to share applications.

> **Smart Tip**
>
> *Tip...*
>
> Traditional classrooms are social: students talk to one another, share ideas, and exchange information. Your online classes also should be social. Provide your students with access to online forums, chat rooms, and message boards to give them an opportunity to meet one another.

Staying In Synch—or Not

Synchronous courses can offer more familiar kinds of instructor-student interactions, which offer great appeal. But they also bring many issues.

You can sell a canned course to as many students as you want, but you can't have an interactive, real-time online seminar with 1,000 students participating at the same time without a huge investment in back-end infrastructure. For the experience to be truly "live," the instructor must be broadcasting video and the students must be equipped to receive it, which requires a broadband connection, a decent PC, and sometimes special software. And it doesn't take too many in class before the virtual raising of hands becomes a problem.

Also, students and teachers often prefer asynchronous e-learning because of the freedom it brings them to work at their own convenience. Compared to driving across town or going on a week-long training mission, being available for an hour or so a day or two a week doesn't seem like asking much. But if it's 2 P.M. Wednesday and your boss just asked you to take care of an emergency, will you really tell him "Sorry, it's time for my class?"

There's a role for both synchronous and asynchronous e-learning, which each come in many flavors and many blends.

Who Can Teach?

Much e-learning fits nicely into a "canned" format—you create the course and students work their way through entirely by themselves. Many IT subjects and

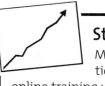

Stat Fact

Most corporations deliver online training via HTML (79 percent), followed by presentation software (33 percent), and Web conferencing (26 percent), according to Forrester Research.

accounting procedures work well this way, for example. But other courses, including almost all for-credit college courses, need an instructor with the proper credentials. The instructor's role changes, especially in asynchronous courses, but is still central. He or she must update course content, run online forums, answer questions from students via e-mail or chat, grade papers, and assume other typical teaching duties.

You must pay instructors on an ongoing basis. You may have to provide them with computer hardware and software and other resources. And—the most difficult part—you have to find them and keep them.

The traditional academic model uses instructors with P.h.D's. It's not unusual for someone to spend years earning a Bachelor's degree, then a Master's degree, then a Ph.D. and accept a teaching position, never leaving academia. More business-oriented learning organizations, like the University of Phoenix, tend to take their instructors from the real world. Their theory is that it's better to learn about business administration from somebody who has run a company than from somebody who has an MBA but has never left the ivory tower.

This is particularly appropriate for business-oriented e-learning content, says Darren Spohn of Spohn Training. Business clients want "a training company that doesn't just have professional instructors, but people who are doing the work as well as teaching people about it."

Getting good instructors is not very different from attracting good employees or contract workers. It hasn't been a problem for Morten Sohlberg of Sessions.edu.

"I already had a pretty good contact net of great instructors, so we started off at a very high level," says Sohlberg. "As we became more known in the industry, it was easier to attract people because we already had a brand name. We didn't have to beg people that had published books to come in and develop courses for us like we had to do in the past."

Sohlberg brings in "thought leaders" and doesn't require an academic background: "They don't need to have previous teaching experience because we have not yet found anyone from academia that has any idea of how to put together a course the way we do."

Likewise, for training seniors in computer basics, Spry Learning in Portland, Oregon, uses the staff at their residential communities

Smart Tip

Count on paying instructors at least $500 per day for their time if you're creating a courseware product, and you want them to help develop and create it. You can get by with a lot less if you're just looking for instructors to teach live classes on an ongoing basis.

and trains them. Spry also develops its own content. At first, it employed gerontologists and instructional designers to develop courses. However, now that it has a "template," Spry can use creative and detail-oriented clerical staff to develop courses.

You might try advertising for instructors on any number of job boards such as Monster (www.monster.com) looking for individuals with teaching backgrounds. Also keep an eye out for "job wanted" classifieds in e-learning newsletters such as the Virtual University Gazette (www.geteducated.com). Generally, you'll want to start them off as freelancers, reducing your administrative and tax payment hassles, and your HR expenses. As you start making contacts, your instructors may know of others they can refer.

Protect Your Property

You may accumulate a great deal of intellectual property within your e-learning company. Intellectual property is different than physical property or the medium over which it is delivered. You can't pick it up and feel it, but you can still own it, and it can't be reused without permission of the owner.

This book, for example, is a piece of intellectual property. It is more than just the paper it is printed on. The real meat of what you bought is the information contained on these pages. Entrepreneur Media owns this information, and you can't reprint it without our permission.

By the same token, if you are offering original material, you must protect yourself against other people taking it. This applies whether you password-protect the information or not. Even if you place it openly on the Web for anybody to see, it's still yours.

When the Internet first started, it was largely an academic exercise and was not used for commerce. Users got the mistaken idea that whatever appeared on the Internet was free for the taking. As a tool of academia, the Internet does indeed make a wonderful venue for the free exchange of ideas. But that is only one purpose. It is also a tool of commerce, and everything is not free.

There may be times when you want someone else to use your material, and you won't want to charge them anything for it. For example, if someone writes a paper on e-learning and uses a sample clip from one of your classes as an example—and speaks highly of it—you'll want to allow that. Similarly, journalists usually may use small clips of text in reviews and articles.

Bright Idea

Every month, go to a search engine such as Google to search the Web for your intellectual property appearing on other Web sites without your authorization. If so, you can issue a Cease and Desist letter; the offending party must either meet your financial terms or stop using your material. Often a simple e-mail message will suffice.

11

It's All About
the Software

An e-learning business runs like any other business. Its product is learning, and it exploits teaching techniques that predate Socrates or were invented last week. But delivering the product is all about the software. Software crammed with content, software enhanced when possible by a live human expert, but software.

An e-learning company belongs to the software community as well as the education community. You don't need to be a programmer. But you do need to be very hip about software and to keep up with e-learning technology as it evolves. And if you're creating content, you must be comfortable managing or otherwise working with software professionals, just as you are with education and content professionals.

Before investing in any particular tool—and especially before betting your business model on a technological edge—make sure you have the financial resources, human capital, and even time to make use of it. And make sure that its deployment won't cut off any large segment of your audience. Don't jump in too far ahead of your audience's willingness or ability to adopt technology.

In this chapter, we'll look at Web sites, software for creating and delivering courses, and collaboration tools including videoconferencing, e-mail, and real-time messaging. We'll also sketch out some technology trends.

Working the Web

You can build a "business card" Web site over the weekend with tools that are probably on your computer or templates from an Internet Service Provider (ISP), who will host a business site for as little as $15 a month. At the other end of the spectrum, a full-fledged site that sells and delivers courses can cost hundreds of thousands to set up plus substantial ongoing expenses to maintain and update.

Wherever you are in this spectrum, you or your designated technical experts want to arm yourself with the massive arsenal of popular Web tools. That includes graphics tools such as Adobe Photoshop, page-creation packages such as Microsoft FrontPage, multimedia tools such as Macromedia Director (for Flash multimedia content), and Adobe Acrobat Reader for distributing high-quality copies of documents.

You also typically exploit standard servers, such as Apache or Microsoft Web servers and SQL Server or Macromedia ColdFusion database servers. You'll also want Web traffic report-ing. If your site is sufficiently complex and often updated, you can check out complete content management systems such as Vignette, although these can be so pricey and your needs so idiosyncratic that you may decide to build your own system. If you have straightforward e-commerce needs, look at off-the-shelf e-commerce services. Depending on how you plan to handle technical support, you also

Stat Fact
About ten million active Internet users in the United States check e-mail or surf the Web for news or local services via mobile phones and handheld computers, according to market research firm ComScore Media Metrix. There are 19 million handheld computer users and 67 million mobile phone users in the United States.

can consider chat-based support tools. You'll often want to rent rather than buy server software, as we'll discuss shortly.

Depending on your business model, you may be able to pass some or all of this heavy lifting off to a business partner, with a link from your site.

For example, MySoftwareHelper offers LearnKey courses from its site that are delivered from LearnKey's servers. Most students don't know or don't care.

This also is a very typical scenario for colleges who frequently contract with a courseware provider for a certain slice of the curriculum. MiraCosta College, for instance, sets up many online services for students on its own Web site. But for online courses, it often finds it more convenient to use the services of the content developer EducationToGo. Students interested in those courses simply link to www.ed2go.com/miracosta, one of many sites EducationToGo has set up for colleges on its servers. It's simple to arrange, and students can take courses in everything from genealogy and creative writing to IT certification courses.

Find a Friendly Host

You'll probably want to use a Web hosting company (also known as an application service provider) during start-up and perhaps indefinitely.

A hosting company maintains your e-learning Web site on its backed-up servers in their climate-controlled server farms. It provides all the back-end security and easily scalable connection options you may need as you grow. For a small- to mid-sized organization, this is very cost-effective. You don't need to shell out for hardware or hire an IT administrator (whose salary may run $60,000 or more). You save time (did you start an e-learning business to deliver education or spend your time tinkering with computers?). You also avoid major headaches—server performance issues, viruses and hack attacks are someone else's problem.

Companies charge as little as $25 a month for hosting, although $100 to 150 is more typical. Amounts climb rapidly depending on the kind of services you use.

Even if you outsource your hosting functions, you or someone in your organization will spend a certain amount of time managing your site on an ongoing basis. It's best if that doesn't require extensive work or technical skills.

Smart Tip *Tip...*

A hosting company makes money by offering standard server platforms and services in a well-defined environment. You must live by its guidelines for security practices, updates, and maintenance. It works with industry-standard software, so if you've built a learning management system on your own database rather than a Microsoft SQL Server or another industry standard, you may be out of luck.

Tools for the Creative Process

E-learning creators use everything from word processors to graphics packages to 3D visualization tools to digital video editors to soup-to-nuts learning management systems that cost corporations millions of dollars each year. Hundreds of vendors offer specialized tools for e-learning. Whether you use that software or create your own, this is the environment in which you live.

If you're creating content, your choice of tools may be entirely dictated by the market you serve. Institutions generally do not want to reinvent the wheel for each course. They would rather take advantage of their existing e-learning infrastructures.

Sell a course to multiple colleges and you are likely to do business with WebCT (www.webct.com) or Blackboard (www.blackboard.com), major players in that market. They each offer not just standard course creation and delivery tools but a supporting suite of communication (such as forums and instant messaging), assessment, administration, and support components. (While definitions can be fuzzy and overlap, these are often described as course management systems, learning content management systems or learning management systems. In general, we'll use learning management system, LMS.)

Similarly on the corporate side, big software and/or training suppliers each promote their own soup-to-nuts e-learning setup package. Their customers shell out for synchronous video courses and other material that demands substantial infrastructure investments. Customers may also buy extensive suites of software that integrate content development (with multiple delivery mechanisms), communications, assessments, administration, support, and other related services. Centra Software (www.centra.com), for instance, offers a rich suite of real-time collaboration applications plus corporate "knowledge management" tools.

Corporations, government, and non-profit institutions all want to preserve their e-learning investments. One aspect of that is to keep content separate from specific delivery platforms, so that it can still be accessed as those platforms evolve or die, or new platforms appear. The Defense Department created the SCORM (Shareable Content Object Reference Model) standard to allow this. Content created for such standards can, at least in theory, be plugged fairly easily into various delivery options: print, Web, PC, handheld computer, and future platform alternatives.

> ## Bright Idea
>
> Make yourself a stack of mini-CDs on which you can store a self-running demo of your software or services. About the size of a business card, these discs nonetheless fit in a standard CD-ROM player and hold more than 5 MB worth of data. They make great leave-behinds for your sales calls or give-aways for trade shows.

E-learning offerings that work over ubiquitous Web browsers and their popular extensions such as e-mail and instant messaging, of course, reach the broadest potential groups of students.

Come Together

You don't do your best learning as a sponge. You learn best by actively interacting with teachers, experts, other students, and other resources.

With sufficient investment in personnel, content, and infrastructure, e-learning can offer this in powerful ways—including some that conventional classrooms can't match. If you go this route, you must, of course, convince your customers on these points.

For live collaboration or a virtual classroom, you at least need a way for students to simultaneously view the same content—whether that's videoconferencing, PowerPoint-like slides, a whiteboard or another application. And the viewing environment needs to be robust enough to give multiple people a way to comment or ask questions in an orderly fashion. It's being done for some classes by many online universities and providers like GlobalKnowledge (wwwglobalknowledge.com).

These technologies are well in hand, assuming you have powerful PCs with high-speed Internet connections. But whether you're creating your own or, in effect, renting conferencing services, they are pricey. There's also a significant learning curve for instructors. Such synchronous learning is probably best applied to IT certification or university courses where course prices can support the cost.

Asynchronous e-learning typically lowers the bar. Student-teacher and student-student communications can happen through the well-established channels of e-mail, chat rooms or bulletin boards.

Here too, however, there's a definite learning curve for you and your instructors. You still must reach out to students in very direct ways to make sure that they enjoy the same kind of give-and-take they would have in a real classroom.

Beyond standard e-mail, you may find a role for an e-mail discussion group, also known as a listserv system. With this, each person's comments are sent via e-mail to the entire group. It's often a part of an e-learning system such as Blackboard. If you aren't using one of these, you can check in a search engine for listserv services like Lyris List Manager (www.lyris.com).

More common is a bulletin or message board, just like the ones sprinkled over the Web except that access is restricted to those in the course. Such online forums

> **Bright Idea**
> Streaming media e-learning can be reused—a session conducted as a live Webinar can be recorded and then rebroadcast over and over as needed.

often spark lively, though slow-motion, discussions, including active participation by some who might stay silent in a physical classroom. A message board is often part of an LMS, and simple versions to add to your site can be found through any search engine.

You may also want to consider adding chat rooms or instant messaging to allow your students to interact with one another or (within certain schedules and limits) the instructor and/or teaching assistant.

e-learning Ecosystems

Course management systems (CMSs) such as Blackboard and eCollege have become virtual fixtures on thousands of college campuses. A combination of interactive learning environment and administrative tools, a CMS enhances the classroom experience and streamlines academic logistics. Learning Management Systems (LMSs) such as Centra Software's Centra or Oracle's iLearning, on the other hand, are e-learning ecosystems more commonly used in corporations.

Both types of environments include most of the same core features. But their names reveal the difference in emphasis, and each generally includes extra tools that more narrowly address the needs of their target audiences. For example, college-bound Blackboard emphasizes behind-the-scenes administrative tools for teachers to set up and administer courses. At this stage in the evolution of e-learning on campus, those are often asynchronous courses.

On the other hand, the highly interactive, real-time meetings that Web environments like Centra and iLearning provide let companies save on travel costs and reduce lost employee work hours.

One of the least-anticipated features of both types of environments is the degree to which they foster student-to-student (or employee-to-employee) as well as student-teacher interaction.

Sharon Senese, a Ph.D. candidate at San Jose State University who lives in San Diego, says the lack of face-to-face interaction with her instructors and other students is the one aspect of traditional classroom instruction that she misses with distance learning. But as a veteran of both Blackboard and numerous other online courses, Senese finds that a class or study group meeting or two per semester fills that gap. In fact, the 24/7 availability of one-to-one or one-to-many communications with Blackboard gives Senese greater contacts with more of her classmates than she might normally get in the typical over-enrolled college course.

>   **Beware!**
> If you're running any sort of chat, online conversation, or message board, there may be a few bad apples participating, possibly subjecting your students to profanity, spam, or just plain harassment. That's why you want a moderated chat or message board, so you can filter out anything inappropriate. Fee-based services and software packages have basic automatic filtering capabilities plus a moderating tool.

Adding either of these technologies to your online educational site need not be difficult or costly. Again, you don't want to reinvent the wheel. There are plenty of chat programs available, many of which are very inexpensive or even free. Instant messaging has spread like Web wildfire, and often replaces e-mail as the main form of Internet connection for those in their teens and 20s. Since major IM systems often don't speak to each other, for now you must take pains to make sure that all your students are on the same IM system if you choose to use that tool.

Again, these tools may be bundled in an LMS. They also are offered by application service providers such as Multicity (www.multicity.com). Make certain that the systems can save and archive transcriptions of your online patter.

Chief Cook and Bottle Washer

Entrepreneurs have a can-do attitude. Good thing, too, because you often must be the chief marketing expert, salesperson and technology guru in the early days.

Can't afford to hire expensive talent to create your Web site? Do it yourself.

Morten Sohlberg, chief executive of Sessions.edu (www.sessions.edu), ran all his Web services from a $600 Macintosh for his first two years in business. Mark Carey of MySoftwareHelper programmed his first Web site himself out of a how-to textbook. For his current, highly transactional and very complicated site, he hired an experienced Web firm after six months of research. It took him awhile to find the right team to fulfill the very specific set of design and operational criteria he had created to ensure that his site was as reliable as it was easy for him to change himself.

Most people can master most tools if they are willing to put in the time like Sohlberg and Carey. The question is, what is the highest and best use of your talents?

Ten Technologies of Tomorrow

The companies who sell technology have a long and distinguished history of portraying each product as a cure-all for just about any business challenge. The press that covers technology often validate that notion, portraying each new development as a fait accompli on announcement day, even though a given technology's benefits may require years of hard work to realize.

E-learning technologies are often great examples of the sizzle being delivered long before the steak. Most of the technologies we are talking about will advance in fits and starts.

That said, here in no particular order are ten technologies (some overlapping) that promise to enhance e-learning.

1. *Software simulations.* You can learn by plunging into a simulation that gives you problems to solve in an environment that's not the real world but does have realistic rules. It works for pilots and surgeons, and it will work for other groups. (Those who can pay the high development costs, that is.)

2. *Expert systems.* We will continue the decades-long quest to build learning systems that guide you to the exact knowledge you need.

3. *Personalized learning.* In related research, learning systems are evolving that study the way you learn best (movies? 3D simulations? text?) and then deliver content accordingly.

4. *Improved assessment methods.* The bottom line for corporate employers is return on their investment in learning. The bottom line for individual workers is certified competence. The bottom line (well, one bottom line) for college students is provable, credential-based achievement. Ways to unobtrusively measure this, in standard ways, will prosper.

5. *DVD.* OK, this is a technology for today, not tomorrow. But the explosive growth of DVDs lets you deliver high-quality video and other high-density material to tens of millions of potential students without worrying about bandwidth constraints. DVD material can be integrated with Web-based content and real-time interactions for hybrid systems that feature the best of both worlds.

6. *Videoconferencing.* Yes, this also is here today. No, it's very far from reaching its potential—in its reach, its quality, and its integration with other e-learning tools.

7. *Interactive TV.* You can offer significant interactions with very limited controls (see the nearest GameBoy for a demonstration). If it spreads in the United States as it has in Europe, interactive TV will offer new opportunities for learning.

8. *Handheld computers and mobile phones.* These offer inexpensive routes to deliver certain kinds of knowledge. In existing pilot programs, for example, school children collaborate to solve math or science programs on handheld computers. In

a simple but useful way, e-books can be read anywhere you go or linked to other learning-oriented content. Mobile phones currently are not as robust platforms as handheld computers, but are adding functionality while being developed at a pace faster than any other consumer electronics category in history. Both platforms benefit immensely from . . . .

9. *Evolving wireless networks near and far.* Connecting via next-generation digital phone networks or wireless nets such as Wi-Fi, both handheld computers and phones will grab significant amounts of learning content from anywhere. Screens and input methods are improving, and there's also a role for learning delivered simply by sound. Which brings us to . . . .

10. *Just-in-time learning.* On today's Internet-connected PCs and tomorrow's handheld devices, e-learning providers aim to deliver learning materials in granular chunks. In a crunch for work or school, you can reach out and learn what you need—no more, no less.

Do you hear a cash register ringing in the distance?

12

Finding the Finances

In this chapter, we'll cover the options for funding your e-learning venture. Will you need to work part time while starting up? Will you exhaust your savings and approach family and friends? Will you seek the participation of well-heeled private investors? Or will you try to hit a home run with venture capital?

Who Are You Going to Call?

The fuel of capitalism is capital. Originally intended by economist Adam Smith to refer to capital equipment—machinery, supplies, and other "real" assets that contribute to productivity—the term now refers to the money you invest to start and expand your business.

Although many a business starts on a shoestring and thrives, many more founder because they don't have enough cash to see them through the start-up phase before revenues regularly exceed expenses.

The start-up period can last years. The larger the idea and the greater the potential reward, the longer the period required to feed a business before it really takes off. A classic example among e-businesses is Amazon.com. This huge success story has generated considerable revenues from the start, but not enough free cash to reward its backers—at least not in the way they envisioned.

Stat Fact

Informal financial support for start-ups was five times that of venture capital support ($300 billion vs. $60 billion) among the 37 most industrialized countries in 2002, according to the Ewing Marion Kauffman Foundation. Nearly one-half of all informal investments are made by family members. While venture capital and IPO totals rise and fall drastically, informal support is more consistently available over time.

While funding sources are limited only by the ingenuity of the entrepreneur, there are four very common ones that are explained in detail in Chapter 4 in *Start-Up Basics*. You may use one or all.

1. *Back-pocket.* Just as it sounds, your first source is always your own cash, savings, inheritance, a home that can be mortgaged, or even a second automobile that can be sold. Many a business has been launched on credit cards, although that is a tremendously bad idea. Most potential investors will want to know that you're putting your own resources on the line before they share theirs.

2. *Friends and family.* These are the folks who know you best. While it will severely test these relationships, this is also a common source of funds for the seed phase of a venture when the basic concept is being hammered out. At the very least, you'll get practice pitching your business plan. Even if your immediate circle doesn't invest, they may tell somebody who will.

3. *Angels.* An "angel" is a wealthy individual who sees value in your concept and who may invest time as well as money in your project. Young entrepreneurs often overlook the value of the former, but an angel with business experience and/or knowledge of your industry can often save you more than money by helping you avoid costly mistakes.

4. *Venture capital.* A venture capitalist is in it for the money. He or she will often want a large equity stake or even partial control of your business in exchange

for bankrolling it. VCs have their choice of deals. They require a rather high minimum investment to make it worth their while and a relatively aggressive exit strategy—that is, a relatively early payback.

There are no unbreakable rules here. Any of these investors might underwrite an e-learning venture at any stage. But venture capitalists are rarely your best choice for the earliest rounds of e-learning financing. They expect to see a very well-honed business plan. They also require strong evidence—perhaps, in the form of a working software prototype or even a revenue stream—that your concept has a potentially large financial payoff.

The availability of venture capital ebbs and flows with the economy, and the surplus of cash available in the late '90s turned into a sustained dry spell after the stock market crash and recession. Of course, that could be interpreted to mean that we're due for an upturn. In any case, financing is only the first of many tests of your persistence and belief in your idea.

Put It on Paper

Entrepreneurs commonly struggle to get others to see what they see. It's as if entrepreneurs are a race of optimists dropped into a land of pessimists. Most people will interpret as insurmountable obstacles the very circumstances that you consider opportunities or welcome barriers to the entry of competitors. Even the most experienced business types are likely to play devil's advocate when approached with an idea that will separate them from their cash for several years.

You must bridge these differences in perspective with your own enthusiasm, commitment, and a written outline of what you plan to do. Even if you're approaching family members, you must commit your vision to paper in such a way that others can see its possibilities.

Two documents that are vitally important to attracting funding at any level are your business plan and an elevator pitch. Take a look at Chapter 3 in *Start-Up Basics* for details on what's needed in a business plan.

Once you have someone interested in your e-learning concept, they'll want to see your business plan up front. Your business plan is not a static document. It's fine-tuned over time as you answer the objections of would-be investors and your understanding of your market steadily grows.

> **Beware!**
> The ultimate red flag for an experienced investor are the words "We have no competition." If you don't now, you soon will. Copyrights or even patents aren't considered substantial protective barriers for an e-learning business. Unique skills or innovative processes for delivering goods or services will be given more credence by potential investors.

An elevator pitch is a very short synopsis of your business plan, so named because it must be brief enough to be presented during an elevator ride. It should be no more than a sentence or two. It should give the basic idea of your business in memorable form. It's designed to build excitement and interest in your concept—to engage the listener enough to make him or her want to read your business plan. Skip the details and highlight your e-learning venture's potential benefits.

> **Smart Tip**
>
> The first thing investors look for in a business plan is an exit strategy—how and when they will get paid. You may just need to give generalities about being acquired or going public. But failure to do so suggests an amateurish insensitivity to an investor's highest priority. The investor likely won't mention what's missing; you just won't be funded.

Show Me the e-Money

Not many of us have an angel investor hanging from the family tree or even in our circle of acquaintances. The solution is to widen the circle, actively networking and seizing every opportunity to find backers.

Or you can immediately turn to the Internet for help. Just typing the words "angel funding" or "venture capital" into a search engine like Google (www.google.com) or AltaVista (www.altavisa.com) will garner you a wealth of possibilities.

Of course, as with most Internet searches, the problem is sifting through the avalanche of responses you'll find. During one recent outing with Google, "angel funding" produced 152,000 results. "Venture capital" coughed up 1.8 million. Most of those hits are duplicates, dead ends, articles where the words "angel" or "capital" appear, or even links to get-rich-quick schemers with a line in the water for the unwary.

But even finance pros will use Internet searches. The good news is that angels and VCs are out there, and they have their own Web pages. The National Venture Capital Association's (www.nvca.org) home page, for example, offers a directory of its 400-plus members. There are West Coast angel networks and East Coast angel networks, and everything in between.

You're still left with a formidable job. But it's a start. And imagine how much better off you are than the entrepreneur of a decade ago who had to, what, look in the Yellow Pages under "Benefactor"?

Also check out the wealth of articles on this topic. *Entrepreneur* magazine (www.entrepreneur.com), for example, has an extensive archive of funding-oriented articles that include tips, suggestions, and contact information for many reliable sources.

Like most things in business, attracting funds is more art than science. It's a highly individualized, sometimes quixotic, pursuit that can't be reduced to boilerplate. But it always benefits from a sprinkling of enthusiasm and even some healthy chutzpah.

Real-World Rainmakers

One place where those qualities can be brought to bear is at a nearby college or university—particularly one with a business school that sponsors plan-writing competitions with seed money for prizes.

"It's not the prize money but the contacts and exposure that make these get-togethers worthwhile," says Joseph Saari, co-founder of Precision Information in Madison, Wisconsin. His company develops software and other educational materials to teach adults about personal finance.

The $4,000 Saari won for third prize in a University of Wisconsin plan-writing competition didn't go far. In fact, Saari gave it all to MBA classmates who helped get his plan ready for competition.

He came away with something far more valuable—a partner and mentor. Ed Harris, the retired founder of a successful Madison software company and a frequent judge in the University of Wisconsin competition, was so impressed by Saari's concept and by Saari himself that he approached the graduate student after the competition. The two agreed to co-found Precision Information.

"Harris, who once ran the 60th largest software company in the nation, is a gift that keeps on giving," says Saari. Now president of Synnovation (www.synnovation.com), which specializes in business consulting for start-ups, Harris has contacts that open sources of funding to Precision and other companies with which he works. He also knows how to go about finding more—on the Web and off.

Perseverance Pays

How bad is the funding environment right now? Not bad enough to keep entrepreneurs down.

Stephen Shank started his online Capella University in Minneapolis under more difficult circumstances. It was 1993, when many people hadn't even heard of the Internet, Web connections were dominated by 14.4Kbps modems, and the dotcom boom hadn't yet happened. He was one of the very first to create such an institution. That made for an exciting start-up phase. Few could understand his business model, and even fewer believed it would succeed. "It wasn't easy to get anybody to provide outside financing to such a concept," says Shank.

Initially, his company was financed by himself and a small-scale venture capitalist who specialized in educational ventures. "The two of us literally boot-strapped this venture from 1993 until 1998, when the concept began to be more plausible to the outside sector," he says.

"By far, the most valuable capital anyone contributes to a business is human capital," says Saari. "Having an experienced team involved and having them willing to work long hours is so much more valuable than having a pot of cash." And potential investors will look closely at your organizational chart and advisory board, notes Harris.

Network and Network Again

Few entrepreneurs bump into a rainmaker in business school or get a yes out of the first angel they pitch. Here's where persistent networking comes in.

Sarah Chapman and Devin Williams, co-founders of Portland, Oregon's, Spry Learning, are also graduates of business schools with business plan competitions. But they attracted angel financing the old-fashioned way, by wearing down shoe leather.

The pair originally set out to find a way to enable seniors in retirement communities to stay in touch with distant family members. But exhaustive research into gerontology and work with seniors in their communities convinced them that there was a burning need to teach seniors over 70 how to use the computer.

While hammering out the special coursework needed and adjusting their business plan, Chapman and Williams became regulars at state and national conventions devoted to gerontology and retirement communities. They began going up to the speakers at these venues (total strangers) and launching right into their elevator pitch.

"You just keep doing it until get your pitch down," says Williams. "The more people you talk to, the more concise your pitch becomes. You learn to get the point across quickly."

After many rejections and referrals, Chapman and Williams finally hooked up with angel investors who understood their sector and whose needs and time frame were compatible with Spry's marketing plan.

"This process can be frustrating and puzzling," says Williams. "Two investors look at the same business plan, and one will say 'I'm concerned about this, but I feel great about that.' The other will have exactly the opposite reaction."

"It depends on their backgrounds and deals they've seen and sometimes a lot of it has to do with personalities," says Williams. "Sometimes you need an icebreaker—unrelated things you might have in common like playing tennis. But, at the end of the day, it behooves an entrepreneur to find someone who has a

Dollar Stretcher

Quicken Premier Home & Business includes a free copy of Palo Alto Software's Business Plan Pro, itself a $100 value. Business Plan Pro is a far cheaper way to create your plan than enrolling in a business school. Then, there's the added benefit of learning how to manage your money with Quicken, which is an education in itself.

background in the things they are interested in and feels some of the same passion."

Williams and Chapman raised a couple hundred thousand dollars in March 2000—not the best of times. They haven't had to raise more yet. Spry Learning reached break-even after its first year of operation and today has annual revenues north of $4 million.

> ## Smart Tip
>
> *Tip...*
>
> Don't forget to work through professional associations (industry, software, or educational) as you network your way toward crucial early investments.

Stretching Exercises

How did Spry Learning turn so little into so much? In very much the same way cited by Precision Information and other successful entrepreneurs: doing more with less.

Spry runs a ten-person company in modest office space, and relies on activities coordinators employed by retirement communities to bring its curricula to seniors.

"Not having a lot of overhead lets you get to break-even quickly before running out of money," explains Williams. "You don't want to be in that position where you need something, and you have to get it. The worse time to raise money is when you need it."

At Precision Information, Saari and Harris agree on this frugal approach. The result is that the three-year-old firm has accomplished a great deal with very little cash. With just a couple hundred thousand dollars, the company has developed a sophisticated educational database that's distributed on CD-ROM via its Web site and as a premium with the products of major partners like Intuit. Custom content also is distributed by other Fortune 500 outfits. Saari figures that Precision has electronically tutored more than one million adults in personal finance, although the company is still in the start-up phase and consists only of its four major equity partners/managers.

Both Spry Learning and Precision Information anticipate the need for limited venture capital soon to finance major expansions. But because both companies have shown they can minimize capital stretch and even produce a self-funding revenue stream, their positions will be considerably strengthened in that negotiation. Already, the equity partners in both companies have given less control to outsiders, and enjoyed more freedom to pursue their respective visions. Ultimately, they will reap greater rewards than if they had accepted venture capital for an unproven concept.

> ## ! Beware!
>
> Don't co-mingle your business and personal funds. Yes, the temptation is great and many start-ups are funded with home equity loans and personal credit cards. But tax troubles lie in wait for those who process receivables through personal accounts. It's a red flag for the IRS, which may even disallow some business deductions on that basis.

They also avoided the excessive amounts venture funds want to invest, and the pressure to grow that puts on management. Chapman and Williams relate the story of another company that was doing something similar and raised $4 million in venture capital.

"We didn't have $4 million, so we were a lot more focused on what we were doing and paid attention to what was working and where we needed to adjust our model," says Williams. "We had a natural discipline that forced us to focus on important things, instead of throwing money at them. This has worked to our advantage."

The rival firm went bankrupt in a year.

The Shoestring Stage

Purse strings loosen up considerably once you can prove that your idea works and generates a revenue stream.

Making a Statement

One of the trickier elements of any business plan is creating the necessary financial statements with three- or five-year revenue projections. Given the uncertainties of business, sales projections are speculative even for established businesses. They're especially challenging to predict before you've really started to make money.

"Venture funders understand this," says Synnovation chief executive Ed Harris. But this is a crucial exercise. While your actual experience will differ, budgets and sales projections do need to be grounded as well as possible in reality.

"Prospective investors are likely to look most closely at your first-year projections," says Harris. He wants to see not too much but not too little allocated for research and development—ideally, 10 to 12 percent. Sales and marketing should account for another 15 to 25 percent, depending on the type of company and its stage of development.

Business school graduates Chapman and Williams of Spry Learning created their own financial models: budget, three-year sales projection, sales strategy, pricing mode, and marketing plan. It helped that they had sales upon which to base their estimates.

If you're not a plan-writing expert, programs such as the $130 Plan Write for Business from BRS Software (www.brs-inc.com) provide standard templates into which you can pour your information. Intuit's Quicken Home & Business and QuickBooks also are chock-full of ready-made financial reports that can be easily adapted to creating suitable projections.

Morten Sohlberg started his New York City Web design e-learning company on a part-time basis. Initially, he resorted to back-pocket funding—partly from necessity, but also to prove to himself that he could do it and that it was something to which he wanted to devote all his energies.

"I have an article from the *New York Post* that wrote about me back then," says the chief executive of Sessions.edu. "They had no faith whatsoever in the Internet as an educational tool. As far as they were concerned, I was a young maniac."

During the early phase, Sohlberg financed his young organization by working elsewhere as a design instructor by day. Likewise, in the early days, Williams and Chapman of Spry Learning lived off savings and outside work. Saari of Precision Information turned down an opportunity to teach at the University of Wisconsin, preferring to deliver pizzas at night so his days would be free for meetings.

Once Sohlberg proved his concept, funding fell into place. "The more evidence you can provide that what you have actually works—not only from a technology perspective but also from a financial perspective—the better," concludes Sohlberg. "The more you can do on a shoestring, the better off you are."

13

Spreading
the Word

This chapter will present an overview of the ways successful e-learning entrepreneurs employ advertising and marketing. How to get your name out to your target audience through public relations and other marketing methods will be explored. And since marketing dollars will be wasted unless you can keep customers, customer service will be looked at too.

These marketing methods are not mutually exclusive. None is necessarily best for you. Over time, you'll figure out which combination is best for your business. Let's hope you can figure that out as quickly and cheaply as possible.

It's an Ad, Ad, Ad World

The Web is the watershed development for e-learning. We all recognize the extent of the opportunity. But recent years have taught us in the most memorable way possible that few companies have yet figured out how to exploit it.

Now that we've gotten viral marketing and pay-per-views, first-mover advantage, and all the other New Economy shortcuts out of our collective system, it's become obvious how little the fundamental principals of good marketing in the virtual world differ from those in the real world. Those who have succeeded have generally followed those principles, mixing viral or other New Economy forms of marketing with more traditional modes of marketing, which you can find discussed at length in Chapter 10 of *Start-Up Basics*.

Still, the Internet is a new medium, offering its own unique set of advertising and other marketing opportunities and challenges over print, radio, or TV.

Company size and geography are no longer as important as they were. Web-based or Web-oriented businesses can reach out to customers around the world—in theory at least, although that can be very expensive. On the Internet, your site is just one of millions. You must figure out inexpensive ways to gather potential customers.

"Traditional marketing is very difficult for education because the audience is very widespread," says e-learning entrepreneur Morten Sohlberg of Sessions.edu in New York City. "It's very hard to pin down the user."

Some e-learning businesses, such as resellers or service firms working with corporate clients, need a presence in their geographical location. Selecting the right advertising vehicle is still tough—as it is for any brick-and-mortar business—but you have a more manageable number of newspapers, specialized publications, radio and TV stations, and mailers from which to choose.

But which, if any, will bring students in the door? Advertising is expensive, and start-ups don't have a surplus of funds.

Mark Carey, chief executive of reseller MySoftwareHelper, alternately advertised on local radio and in local computer newspapers and law journals. These did not prove effective. "We tracked the calls from print ads through our Web site, and I don't think I got one bit of business out of all that radio and print advertising," says Carey. "I got a couple of calls, but not one close. The ads were creative, they were flashy, they were cute. But they just didn't pay off."

> **Beware!**
>
> Web banner ads are often sold by cost-per-thousand (CPM)—or how many times the page is viewed. But views alone aren't that fruitful. You care more about how many people actually click on your ad—the click-through rate. You care most, of course, about those who actually buy. Be sure to analyze traffic on your Web site to see what's working.

Name a target market and you'll find that your friendly local ad sales representative has no trouble at all demonstrating statistically that his or her media outlet reaches those individuals. But advertising is art, not science. As in Carey's case, the only way to find out whether a particular advertising outlet pays off for you is to try it.

And throwing up a single ad won't do it. You must try not just once but over a decent period of time. Advertising is about persistence, not just reach. You pay based on cost-per-thousand impressions (CPM), but people rarely buy the first time they see an ad. Usually, they must see your message many times before they get a sense of your permanence and the impulse to buy is translated into action.

"If you're going to advertise, you need pretty deep pockets to pound away month after month after month," says Carey, "and most small businesses can't afford that."

Assuming you have found the right venue for your audience, getting the response you want depends on a number of other factors—your message, the creative quality of your ad, the time of day or even the season it is delivered, and even outside events.

Being creative helps, but sometimes, you just can't be creative enough. Think of SuperBowl TV ads—some people find them as entertaining as the game itself, but only rarely does lightning strike so that they pay off.

In the Virtual World

As difficult as it is to craft a good local advertising campaign, it's even tougher to get a good return on ads if, say, yours is an IT certification business or online university whose students may come from all across America. Yes, the University of Phoenix (www.phoenix.edu) spends massively on online ads for its online courses. But a start-up doesn't enjoy that option.

As Sohlberg points out, the Internet is inherently global in focus. Even though a banner ad, pop-up, or other Web advertising technique may seem to have a low CPM compared to other venues, they reach vast numbers of people you don't care about.

> **Tip...**
>
> **Smart Tip**
>
> Run traffic analysis software on your Web site so that you can keep tabs on what type of visitors you get, which pages they look at, which links or offers they respond to, how long they spend on the site, where they come from, where they go, and other important statistics.

Unless your target audience is nearly universal, buying a basic ad on a main page on a site like Yahoo! isn't cost-effective. Yahoo! will be only too happy to place the ad. It's a high-traffic site that probably does a good job for consumer product or lifestyle companies. But its top pages will scoop up a lot of viewers who don't match up with your market. You'll be casting your net too wide, spending money on many people who won't be able to take advantage of your services by virtue of geography or interest.

Instead, you want to pick a specific page on Yahoo!—say, the directory page for the "Distance Learning/Computers" page or the page that comes up when you search on "IT certification."

> ## Smart Tip
>
> If you want to place a banner ad on a Web site, you'll be quoted a CPM rate or cost per 1,000 visits. Here's how to calculate how much it costs you to attract each visitor to your site with your ad. With 100,000 visits and a click-through rate of 0.4 per 1,000 visits, you get 40 visits. If your CPM is $2, the ad costs $200, so each visit costs $5.

Speaking of search, it may be very effective to pay for premium placement in the Web's major search engines like Google, AltaVista, AllTheWeb.com, Inktomi, and Teoma. Basically, you pay to be in the first few listings that come up with searches on different keywords. This is the only type of advertising Mark Carey of MySoftware-Helper uses now, and he says that it provides good results. Some search engines focus on particular topics or communities.

Each engine operates a little differently, but Google is one of the most popular engines. A Google site page (www.google.com/ads/overview.html) will tell you everything you need to know about this kind of advertising.

Want a consultant to help you get prime search engine placement? Contact Overture (www.overture.com). Want a list of all the search engines on the Net? Type "search engine" in any of them—or visit the e-zine SearchEngineWatch (www.search enginewatch.com).

The other main approach, of course, is to find a narrower site that's more likely to be visited just by individuals in your target market group. If you're an online university or IT training company, it might be an education portal like Colleges.com (www.colleges. com) or eLearners.com (www.elearners.com). If you are targeting knowledge-workers, try a job board such as Monster.com (www.monster.com). Even here, you may be casting your net too widely.

The goal is to find a site that delivers the combination of content related to yours, proven high traffic, and responsiveness of visitors. What works for you may be highly individual. It's important to track how many times your ad is clicked, and how far those visitors continue into your site. The basic measure is reasonably straightforward: Did you get some business?

Web advertising and marketing don't easily reduce to broad generalizations. They need to be seasoned with a little common sense and, again, trial and error that varies with your type of business.

In the case of IT certification, the number-one place that professionals go to find e-learning providers is the equipment vendor's Web site, according to Apex InfoTech in Irvine, California. It gets most of its business from the Microsoft Web site. Apex doesn't even pay for most of those referrals. It's just on a list of authorized trainers that Microsoft provides for Web visitors.

Don't forget that if your ads do start to pay off, you must be thoroughly prepared to respond quickly and effectively, whether that means taking questions and orders over the phone or kicking off actual product delivery on the Web.

Telling the PR Story

There are other ways to get your message out, including public relations.

Here the goal is to get your company's name in the media without having to pay for it. For that reason, it's sometimes referred to as "free advertising." But while you don't pay directly for the coverage, PR is neither free nor easy to come by.

PR specialists try to generate interest among journalists on your behalf by presenting them with newsworthy information that is relevant to the publication, and you'll pay them for the hours they spend doing it. You may be surprised at their low rate of success. It isn't a reflection on the PR folk necessarily, but rather, the difficulty of the task. The staff on most publications and broadcast shows spend a lot of time planning and weighing the impact of different stories, and it isn't that easy to get in synch with their editorial plans if you're an outsider.

PR is worth the effort. Let's say you do have "a story." Your public relations advisor might try to interest an educational publication with a lengthy piece about your content. But you also could try to interest a financial magazine in running a short piece about your venture funding, or a business magazine in your start-up experiences, or a technology magazine about some aspect of your delivery strategy.

On the plus side, high-tech media are relatively plentiful, and the general business press very amenable to tech-related stories (often more so than to education stories per se). Also, newspapers and news-oriented magazines and the electronic media with high frequencies and huge appetites to fill may be easier to get into.

Dollar Stretcher

You may be able to go cheaper by hiring a PR agency for individual projects, as opposed to the monthly retainer that they prefer. You may have to shop around a little, but the agency must account for each hour it bills.

> **Smart Tip**
>
> If you do computer training, join a computer user group or two, and give free presentations at meetings. They are all over America and a great way to heighten your profile and establish your expertise. In major urban centers, you can probably find a user or other affinity group that closely matches the demographics of your target audience.

Even so, your PR representative will need a little luck and fortuitous timing. Public relations typically requires a lot of hard-scrabble legwork and cold calls to establish media contacts, put your name out in front of the media, and keep it there so that when a story on a related topic comes up, the journalists will think of you.

If you do get the press to write favorably about you, however, it can be more beneficial than a dozen ads. Since this is a recommendation of sorts from an independent third party, it usually carries considerably more value with the audience than an ad. Having *Time* magazine devote a page to the efficacy of your training would be thousands of times more beneficial than a dozen ads in *Time* (which, naturally, you can't afford).

Also, PR is about overcoming inertia. A story in *Time* would, in all likelihood, be the first pickle out of the jar for you. Your PR representative would use it as a testimonial to get attention from other media. Spry Learning in Portland, Oregon, was lucky enough to get an article on its seniors training early on in the *Los Angeles Times*. It resulted in numerous other press contacts and profiles on the company, which it uses as testimonials on its Web site. This process can work in reverse, too: Reporters on big publications may follow up on a story they spot in more specialized publications.

Public relations firms will want you to sign up for a monthly retainer that could easily be $3,000 to $5,000. Their hourly rates can easily range from $50 to $200, depending on the seniority of the individuals involved in your campaign and the type of campaign it is. It might just be a simple press release announcing your existence or a backgrounder on your company. It might be one of those ongoing campaigns to keep putting your name out in front of the media.

During start-up, however, try to hire well-connected individual freelance PR people for about $60 to $100 per hour. A one-person show won't necessarily have all the resources of a full-fledged PR firm—maybe not all of the marketing savvy and planning resources and staffers ready to launch a campaign. But that may be all you need until you get the ball rolling. You can find these people through your extensive ongoing business networking. Get samples of their work and check out their references.

You also can do your own PR. The founders of Spry Learning combine market research with good PR by becoming experts on seniors training at as many trade shows and conferences as they have time for. Mark Carey of MySoftwareHelper also makes numerous presentations and sometimes appears on local radio or public TV stations as an educational expert. Other chief executives stay in touch with key media contacts by phone or e-mail; many even give "virtual press tours" by Webinar.

A Welcome Site for Customers

Before we leave the topic of advertising and public relations, let's talk again about your best marketing buy—your own Web site. It's both an advertising and PR vehicle.

As we know, a Web site is your own personal billboard alongside the information superhighway. Granted, it's a highway broader than the Amazon River, and every inch of space on either side is crowded with similar billboards. But it costs you so little to put up a basic billboard, and the display advertising aspect is only the start of its usefulness.

Your Web site will be, in a sense, the central clearinghouse for all your marketing efforts, a cheap way to distribute information to potential customers and the most convenient place for them to connect with you.

You'll include your URL on your business cards, stationery, marketing material, packaging labels, merchandising giveaways, and in any ads you place elsewhere. Your URL will probably become more important than your street address and telephone number.

Most good dotcom domain names are taken. But even if you do manage to snag a URL in the ".com" domain, you also should make sure that yours is the site on which Web surfers are most likely to land by also registering your URL in the more recently opened dot.biz and dot.us domains. Depending the nature of your business, you may even fit in the dot.edu or dot.pro domains. It's worth a try at the very least. Each registration will cost $25 to $50 a year—pretty cost-effective even if you only get one customer out of it.

You might be able to pay for that by becoming an associate of other Web sites—that is, providing them with referrals that turn into business for them. For example, educational courseware developer LearnKey pays its associates $15 for every sale it makes from a referral—that's $15 for every course sold, not just $15 per customer.

Likewise, you'll want to get a link to your site in the link lists of as many related sites as you can. LearnKey gets 100,000 visitors a month to its Web site (www.learnkey.com). Get in the newsletters of related sites—either through advertising or PR (being an education expert). You may even want to advertise on a site like LearnKey.

Remember to keep an eye on your site, to make sure it's up and running effectively, and respond quickly to any e-mail or other messages it generates.

> **Tip...**
>
> ## Smart Tip
>
> Want a good Web site model? Nielsen/NetRatings (www.nielsen-netratings.com) measures the top 25 Web sites each week. The sites can afford the best and brightest Web page designers and marketers to work on them. You can get good design hints and traffic-building ideas from them.

Getting Sticky

In addition to finding a way to rise above the clamor and clutter of the Internet, you want to make the most of the visitors who do land on your site. Good graphics and an easily navigable site are important, of course. But they are really just the ante in the game. They aren't really what holds people once they're on your site or make them buy.

Demos of your courses will help—people want to check out the product. And the more time they spend with you, the more likely they are to make a connection.

You want to have a "sticky" Web site. Stickiness refers to techniques or features that hold people on your site, get them to navigate around and investigate more deeply, and keep them coming back. They don't necessarily come back every time to buy something. But every time they return to your site, they are exposed to what you offer. The longer and more often they are exposed, the more likely they are to spend money.

Making your Web site "sticky" may mean giving away something for free in hopes of selling something else. You might do it by offering a series of free short courses, which serves the purpose of introducing students to your site. As they continually revisit your site to see what you are giving way, you can promote the fee-based ones as well.

Another very common way to do this is through an informative monthly e-mail newsletter. Offer it for free, but get more than e-mail addresses of your customers if possible. The newsletter can push your fee-based offerings, naturally.

Another way to maximize the business you get from each customer is with an online incentive or loyalty program, much like the loyalty programs of supermarkets and airlines. You set up an array of awards for behaviors you want to encourage in your Web site visitors. There are many ways to approach it; a very common one is to set up a frequent buyer/visitor rewards program that doles out points that eventually earn visitors discounts or prizes—maybe from your site, often from the sites of your partners.

Assign points when customers buy products, of course, but also by amount. They can get points when they register online, fill out a market survey, or refer a friend who registers (which is often referred to as viral marketing). You also can dole out points for various holiday promotions. It's a simple enough program to set up in-house. But you can also outsource your program to a company that offers turnkey points programs such as MyPoints.com (www.mypoints.com).

Beware!
If you plan to use an e-mail newsletter to keep new and current students coming back to your Web site, make sure that it's the opt-in variety. You can send them an invitation, but don't distribute marketing materials to just any e-mail list. People's patience for spam is already sorely tested.

Show Your Stuff

Depending on your type of e-learning business, shows may be a better source of students than any other marketing method. Trade shows (local, regional, and national), conferences, seminars, professional association meetings, and other meetings all let you get your name and face out in front of the public.

As with everything else, only select shows will work for you. An e-learning trade show may be informative, but if dominated by people just like you, it may or may not generate customers.

Selection isn't always obvious. Mark Carey of MySoftwareHelper has had his best marketing success at the Seattle I-Tech show, a local version of a nationwide show series. But Carey also has enjoyed success at selling to Indian tribal councils.

Spry Learning, which targets seniors, attends the annual conferences for the Assisted Living Federation of America and the American Association for Homes and Services for the Aging as well as the affiliated state conferences, and senior housing conferences for governmental organizations.

"With conferences, you have a concentration of hundreds or thousands of people—experts in the industry," explains Spry co-founder Devin Williams. "You can make presentations of your own, listen to speakers, and talk to people in the industry. It's a good way to get both information and attention."

Even when they don't exhibit, MySoftwareHelper and Spry make trade shows pay off by presenting in the seminars.

Running a booth like LearnKey's can be expensive. You can easily spend between $10,000 and $50,000 for a high-profile trade show appearance—not just space, but staffing and merchandising materials, and perhaps a reception or two. There are creative firms that specialize in creating effective trade show displays and events, and they can cost you thousands of dollars themselves. But there are cheaper ways to go, too, starting with the size and design of your booth and the number of people who attend from your company.

Not every square foot of trade show floor space costs the same. Giant LearnKey often commands a good deal of booth space at the shows it attends. MySoftwareHelper and Spry maintain a lesser profile farther out toward the edges of the trade show floor. There's also space available in smaller booths along the show floor perimeter—the cheap seats. Devin

Smart Tip

Learn the ins and outs of trade show exhibiting at The TradeShow Coach (www.TheTradeShowCoach.com). This Web site includes articles, books, tapes, workshops, and free weekly e-mail tips.

Williams figures that a booth for two days costs between $800 and $1,800. It costs Spry around $5,000 to go to national shows, but it often can get by for under $2,000 at smaller, regional shows.

Both the leads generated and the notoriety generated can take awhile to pay off. "You can recoup that, but it doesn't necessarily happen the first year you do it," says Williams. "It's very good exposure—people start thinking about it and when they start talking about it, your name comes up, and people start to refer to you."

Both Williams and Carey agree that trade show benefits are not always immediate—that you sometimes get referrals that take three to nine months to realize. A part of that relates to the long sales cycle for the customers of both Spry and MySoftwareHelper training. Williams figures that retirement centers to which she markets take about nine months to make up their minds.

Word-of-Mouth

Whatever your business, you need excellent customer service, which generates favorable word-of-mouth. So, you can think of word-of-mouth marketing and customer service as two sides of the same coin.

Good reputations don't happen overnight and can't be bought with ads and press releases. Yes, other marketing efforts start the process, but good reputations can be sustained only by delivering on a promise.

When you come recommended, the sale is a done deal. As you start building up a customer base, you'll want to make sure that their every experience with you and your

Directly Speaking

Direct mail and direct e-mail can be very effective in gaining new customers and getting repeat customers—if you target your market correctly.

In direct e-mail marketing, this is especially important because of the sensitivity Internet users have to being "spammed," or sent unsolicited e-mail advertisements.

Targeted e-mail, on the other hand, is very effective, especially when it is delivered to an "opt-in" audience. This is an audience that has previously expressed a desire to receive e-mail announcements of a certain type, sometimes in exchange for a premium, such as signing up for a free newsletter.

employees is favorable. That usually means going above and beyond the call to make sure that the customer has a good experience.

"Here is where a lot of companies fall short," says Mark Carey of MySoftware-Helper. Carey worked with an ad agency to come up with post-sales collateral materials to help companies show potential students how to get to the product.

Part of customer service is customer relationship management, which means actively nurturing the relationship you have with each customer—cross-selling, if you can. Always give them more than they can get from your competition. To do this, study their preferences and anticipate their needs. You never know when some action on your part will lead to an unanticipated sale.

Spread Your Merchandise

Try a marketing method that can be employed relatively cheaply in both the real and virtual worlds: merchandising. Merchandising is something you do to entice new students, hold onto current students, or get them to buy up without cutting your prices and devaluing your brand.

It can be used in conjunction with both your advertising and PR as well as your effort to make your Web site sticky. To take one rather prosaic example, you could offer a virtual gift certificate on your Web page for visitors who bring you a successful referral. The gift could be an introductory course or courseware or a prize you've worked out with another site—say, $10 worth of merchandise on an electronics Web site.

At the very least, you're likely to capture marketing information on both the referrer and referee through your merchandising efforts. You can make the gift certificate a part of your advertising and PR materials. It might put an immediacy to your ad that gets people moving. You can also use it to build traffic at your trade show booth.

Here again, having a Web page saves you money over traditional real-world merchandising methods (not that they don't also have merit). Your virtual gift certificate is better than a paper one because there are no printing or distribution costs involved. You can change your materials in five minutes in response to the action you're seeing without incurring printing costs all over again.

A classic example: The Bay Area's Le Boulangerie bakery chain offers instant online coupons for a pastry to those who log onto the Web using its wireless LAN hotspots.

Customer service is considered a cost center by most large companies, who seem more willing to invest in elaborate call centers and technology than in individuals who can really help. A start-up that handles service more personally can generate pleasant memories for customers.

Good customer service is easy to say, easy to put in your press releases, but hard to fulfill. The good news is that you can stand out and generate good word-of-mouth by providing real customer service.

14

Failure
and Success

This chapter discusses the elements of success for entrepreneurial ventures, and help to provide insights that aid in getting your e-learning business off the ground.

We'll also share the hard-won wisdom of several of the entrepreneurs whom we interviewed for this book and just a few of the ways they ensure small victories that add up to long-term success.

Rocky Road

Recent economic events are just the kind of lemons from which entrepreneurs have always made lemonade. If we hop back a couple of decades, we find a very similar set of economic circumstances—actually, a much more onerous set of conditions. But it was from double-digit inflation, double-digit interest rates, and tight capital that the latest entrepreneurial revolution sprang.

The intervening 20-plus years have created a bumper crop of entrepreneurs never before seen. They were years of nearly unbroken progress with vast increases in American wealth, leapfrogging productivity improvements, the taming of consumer

---

GEMs of Wisdom

The Global Entrepreneurship Monitor (GEM), funded by the Ewing Marion Kauffman Foundation, studies entrepreneurship and economic growth in 37 countries and identifies entrepreneurs as adults aged 18–64 involved in the start-up process or engaged as the owner/manager of a business less than 3½ years old. Here are some findings from ongoing entrepreneurial research, with some surprises.

- More Americans are trying to create new companies than new marriages or babies.
- Despite strides made by female entrepreneurs, men are still about twice as likely to start new ventures as women.
- Individuals aged 25 to 44 are the most active age group entrepreneurially.
- African-American men and women are about 50 percent more likely to start a business than Caucasian men and women, and those rates rise sharply with education levels.
- Rates of entrepreneurship rise significantly with levels of education, especially among minorities. Black and Hispanic men with post-graduate experience are at least twice as likely to be involved in a start-up than white men with similar education.
- Most entrepreneurs work in teams of about two people, but about 40 percent work alone.
- In the United States especially, new companies are more likely to be formed by people who have jobs, rather than by those who have been laid off.

inflation, and the lowering of interest rates to the point where capital is readily available to U.S. businesses and consumers.

What did it? You, and your neighbors, relatives, friends, and acquaintances who have been innovating and creating new products and processes.

As important as its activities may be, government doesn't create wealth. It doesn't come up with new ideas. It doesn't invent new, more efficient manufacturing, service, or managerial processes. It doesn't open factories or invest in product research.

Government actions do not move the needle on the national productivity scale, which is the source of new wealth that permits the creation of new jobs. Government just lays the groundwork for others to do that.

Those that do move the needle are typically relatively young, relatively small companies. That's where the most innovation takes place. That's where most jobs and new wealth are created each year.

So, here we are and there you are, without the advantages of a cozy relationship with a regulatory agency, or a golden parachute, or a diversified product line and market dominance. You have to do things the hard way—from scratch. You have seemingly insurmountable obstacles and many long workdays in front of you. You need to play for real money in a game whose rules you may not know and are always changing.

Yes, You Can

You can succeed anyway, like millions of entrepreneurs before you.

That's not to minimize your individual challenges. You can't know in advance what they will be, what the right answer to them will be, or whether they will turn out to be opportunities in disguise. But success never travels alone. It's always accompanied by challenges, with new ones springing out of your solution to old ones. No one ever succeeded without them. But you can do it.

"When I started the company two years ago, I knew nothing about e-learning, had no contacts, and had no clue where to start," recalls Mark Carey of MySoftwareHelper.

Actually, the slope was steeper than that for Carey. About the time that he decided he was tired of all the travel involved in being national sales manager for a large drug company, Carey's wife died, leaving him with their two little girls. In addition, there were legal complications that tied up all the family's assets—from insurance policies and mortgages right down to Carey's car registration and line of credit. A career change is a challenging period in just about anyone's life.

Stat Fact
The number of Americans in entrepreneurial activities reached an all-time high of 16.6 percent of the population in 2000 and now has stabilized at around 10 percent, according to the Ewing Marion Kauffman Foundation.

> **Stat Fact**
> About 286 million of the world's people, or 12 percent of the 2.4 billion-person labor force in the 37 most industrialized nations, are involved in new business formation, according to the Ewing Marion Kauffman Foundation.

But we can only guess at the additional emotional turmoil and complications involved in such a loss.

Eventually, Carey worked out the family finances and scraped together enough money to do the research and development for his business. He managed to interest an angel investor in his venture and was counting on that individual to provide the $250,000 needed to launch MySoftwareHelper. But the day Carey was to sign the contract to have his Web site developed, the angel backed out.

"I thought, 'I've done all this work and I'll be damned if I am going to let this die,'" Carey recalls. He cashed in his stock options from his previous job, found a cheaper Web developer and ad agency, and pushed on.

When Carey first started calling on companies to sell e-learning courseware, many were already locked into multi-year contracts with competing courseware companies who had broad but not complete lines. So he started his relationship with many companies by selling a single course that the other courseware provider didn't offer. Then, through diligent client service, he has convinced companies to convert to his courses.

"Find a niche that your competitor isn't filling and go after that part of the business," advises Carey. "Find something customers need, and start building trust in your product line."

MySoftwareHelper is hugely successful. Asked why he chose e-learning when he had no previous experience in education, Carey responds: "Why should that stop anybody? If you have an idea and know how to market yourself, it doesn't matter about your experience."

Don't Quit Until You Hit

New businesses require tremendous up-front effort without immediate return. You must develop your market, and often with many early disappointments. Many have followed the "Build It and They Will Come" approach and found that customers didn't come. Many more quit before the customers discovered them.

You'll need enough money to see you through. And you very well may need one or more mid-course corrections.

"The thing that has kept me going and knowing that I will succeed and break out is that there have been a lot of successful people before me and not one of them had it easy," says Carey. "Not one of them maxed out this opportunity. I just know it will work."

Never be satisfied. So you made a sale? Where is your next one coming from? While you keep looking for new customers, remember that usually the least costly sale you can make is to the individual you just sold. Sell them a more expensive version of the e-learning content they just bought or content on another topic.

> **Smart Tip**
> It requires discipline, but if you're sure you'll pay off the balance every month, you can enhance your cash flow by paying all suppliers with a credit card. You get the 28 days of float from the card company and tons of frequent flier miles that can offset business travel expenses.

And market to their colleagues and friends. "Results from cold calls begin to dwindle after awhile," says Carey. "Every single sale we make, I always ask for testimonials and I always ask if they know someone else."

Carey knows of one Washington school district that uses six courses to teach Microsoft Word. Each department bought their courses individually from a different company. Not only will Carey try to convert all of them to his particular brand of courseware, but now that he knows how things work in that district, he will aim to find out what other courses are used by what departments and not by others.

Carey never completes installation of a new corporate e-learning system without asking the customer for contact information of other people in other departments or companies. He then calls on them, confident that the name he drops will give him a good recommendation. "I use testimonials to sell more companies from the Web site. But if I sell a law firm, I call others and say, 'I just sold this course to so-and-so, and I understand that you may have a need for the same training. Would you be interested in sitting down and chatting?'"

Of course, the person making the original recommendation should be entirely happy with your offering. If the new sales prospect calls to check, you need a glowing recommendation.

You'd Be Surprised

You never know where a sale will take you. Carey took a shot and sold a management skills course to an Indian tribe for use among their casino employees. He was then invited to make a presentation at the national tribal council because one satisfied and influential tribal member recommended his company to the national organization.

On the other side of the coin, Carey got pretty excited when Microsoft asked MySoftwareHelper to help put together a CD with a compilation of tech courses that Microsoft could send free to 250,000 Microsoft technical newsletter subscribers. The CD would be branded with MySoftwareHelper links and logos and information on how to get to its Web site. Carey figured that, if only 1 percent of 250,000 subscribers bought a course at $500 apiece, he'd generate $1.25 million in revenue.

"I figured this would be unbelievable," he recalls. "We were standing by the phones, but the phones didn't ring. What I learned is nothing is as big as you think it's going to be. There was no big bang. Calls trickled in over a period of months. Out of that, we probably generated $50,000 of revenue."

It did lead to other, more profitable ventures with Microsoft, however.

First-Mover Advantage

Stephen Shank's biggest challenge when he set out to start his online university in Minneapolis in 1993 was that it was 1993. The Internet as we know and love it today did not exist. The idea of a university online was unproven.

Shank's second challenge was to get the accreditation necessary for regulatory approval from the state licensing agency and federal government. At the time, both were very skeptical of the concept of e-learning; it was a radical idea for most people. Fortunately, early pioneers like Shank blazed a trail so that it's easier for later entrepreneurs.

OK, so it's far too late for you to be the first online university. But e-learning is far from mature. There is some way to innovate in your market. There is something your customers need that isn't being provided by others.

IT Skills Loan (www.itloan.com) provides education loans of from $3,000 to $20,000 to IT students, including loans for computer equipment. IT Skills Loan isn't the first company to make loans, it isn't even the first company to make education loans. But it adds value through a deep understanding of the particular needs of this market. It markets through school financing administrators. Its lending policies are more flexible with IT students in that they are more willing to fund the training than, say, the Bank of America.

KnowledgeNet is a nationwide provider of business skills training to corporate executives through a number of venues, including its KnowledgeNet Live synchronous training over the Internet (www.knowledgenet.com). That's fairly distinctive by itself. But KnowledgeNet knows that we are social creatures and goes a step further. Some students need the instruction mixed with a level of personal interaction similar to a traditional classroom, so KnowledgeNet augments both its synchronous and asynchronous classes with a mentor program whereby students can get personalized instruction online from experts in different subjects. That's particularly important for seekers of IT certifications who need counseling.

These details matter. Execution can be as important as the original idea. You don't have to invent the wheel. You just have to give your customers something better than they can get it elsewhere.

Don't Forget the Check

Unlike many older educational institutions, you won't get funding from the government. And no one will float a bond issue if you run short of cash. You may be a natural-born business leader, teacher or content creator, but you also have to close the sale.

Whatever else you are doing and whatever your previous work history, you are the number-one salesperson for your business.

And how do you do that? "The most effective tools a sales representative can have are to have good listening skills and be creative," Carey says. You often must be creative just to get your foot in the door, but once in, you have to know in what direction to take your creativity. Forget the canned sales pitch. Listen to your customer, find what they need, and deliver creative ways to satisfy those needs.

Morten Sohlberg of Sessions.edu reminds us that the traditional brick-and-mortar model of academia simply doesn't apply to e-learning. "Although we are a real educational company, we also very much have a bottom line," he notes. "We're a real company here to create an extraordinary user experience. But we need to make money. It's as simple as that. The way we operate our business will be very similar to any other business."

That means not forgetting to ask for the check. And keep asking when needed.

You also want checks coming at you from more than one direction. As in any entrepreneurial venture, you want multiple revenue streams since many markets go through boom times and bad as well as responding to the seasons of the year. How many classes, for instance, could you schedule for the week between Christmas and New Year's?

Examples of alternate revenue streams might be selling courseware as well as teaching courses, selling books that go along with courseware through your Web site, and arranging affiliate relationships with other Web sites to get paid for referring Net surfers to them.

Once you enter a market, there typically will be many subtle opportunities, some of which may even trump your original business model.

Take Precision Information. It mass-markets CDs of its "Encyclopedia of Personal Finance." It also sells these discs to wholesale buyers who then use it to educate different customer groups. Additionally, Precision will customize a portion of the content for financial service firms

Smart Tip

Need to cast a nationwide marketing net for your IT certification training school? You can advertise or pay to get premium position in the search engines of IT Web portals like Find Computer Schools (www.find-computer-schools.com). This has a powerful database of IT certification training resources searchable by training type, topic, certification type, state, ZIP code, and numerous other parameters.

Stat Fact

One sales point is straightforward: Sixty-seven percent of respondents to a training survey cited cost savings as the most important benefit they derive from online training, according to Forrester Research.

such as Ameritrade, Morningstar, and New York Life that focus on just a portion of the subject matter. And it licenses blocks of its content to consultants providing financial education to other groups.

"It's important for any company to have multiple revenue streams, and we planned it as well as we could from the start," says Precision chief executive Joe Saari. "But you never fully understand how they will evolve. You can never tell which will grow fastest or which revenue stream will turn out to be the richest vein. But they all leverage one another, and we know that we definitely want complementary revenue streams."

What's an Entrepreneur?

Are you a teacher, a programmer, a computer geek or an entrepreneur? Whatever it is that motivated you to embark on an e-learning venture, you probably lack the full range of skills needed for success. You simply want to try to leverage those skills and find colleagues who will fill in the gaps.

Relevant experience is always good, but there is no particular educational or employment background that qualifies or disqualifies you from participating in the e-learning market.

More important is to possess that indefinable quality of entrepreneurship. You make the leap. You put in the hours. You make the tough decisions.

The Ewing Marion Kauffman Foundation has been studying entrepreneurs worldwide statistically and qualitatively since 1992. Its intent is to learn enough about entrepreneurs to make policy suggestions that foster entrepreneurship.

Unsurprisingly, the Kauffman Foundation has found that the level of entrepreneurial activity in the United States and the world generally mirrors changes in the growth of each nation's gross domestic product. The real numbers of entrepreneurially active individuals worldwide keeps increasing. And despite recent tough times, the Kauffman Foundation believes that we are entering another period of upswing for entrepreneurship.

"The U.S. has stabilized at a level of entrepreneurial activity that will allow us to begin rebuilding or at least maintaining our current position for some time," says Larry Cox, director of research at the Kauffman Foundation.

Entrepreneurs like you cut across every socio-economic and racial classification in both the United States and the world. You can't be pinned down like butterflies on velvet. By definition, you are surprising and counter-intuitive. You see opportunity where most of us see problems. You persevere when logic counsels retreat. You are a creator, and you are probably born to that role. You will get reshaped and tempered by the ventures in which you get involved. You'll need that flexibility in e-learning as much as any other venture.

You buck the odds. You have a dream itching to be fulfilled, so much so that you can't be content with a safe job. You have fire in the belly. You are a natural risk-taker.

Each entrepreneur takes a different path. The Kauffman Foundation's ongoing surveys demonstrate that there is no one right way to start a company, no step-by-step process—not even similar starting points for most entrepreneurs. Instead, it's all about recognizing opportunities, figuring out solutions, and working through the hurdles to realize your goal.

> ## Smart Tip
>
> If you sell e-training to a corporation or government agency, there may be a large initial opportunity, but it slows down. Eventually, almost all employees experience the courses they need (there's turnover, but usually at low rates). But if you sell to even one educator, you will get new sales every quarter or semester, since that's how often students turn over for a class.

Whatever avenue of entrepreneurship you choose, be sure that you're doing something day in and day out that gives you pleasure and the kind of psychic rewards we all seek. Then at least, succeed or fail, it will have been a profitable experience.

As Joe Saari of Precision Information puts it: "Do something you love, and you'll never work another day in your life."

Appendix
e-Learning Business Resources

You've heard this saying: "Everything I know I learned in kindergarten." Yes, it was written by someone who grew up before the Internet.

Just about everything you ever knew or may want to know can be found on the Internet. It is the newspaper, magazine, and database resource of record for modern information.

Nowhere is that truer than for the topic of e-learning. Type that word or any of its synonyms into any Web search engine and you will have a lifetime's worth of information to peruse. If we were to publish only the names and addresses of education-related Web sites, it would probably take a publication the size of the one you have just finished reading.

We'll leave it to you to lasso those areas of most interest to you. But here are some e-learning resources to get you going.

Accreditation

Middle States Association of Colleges and Schools, for Delaware, District of Columbia, Maryland, New Jersey, New York, Pennsylvania, Puerto Rico, Virgin Islands, www.msache.org

New England Association of Schools and Colleges, for Connecticut, Maine, Massachusetts, New Hampshire, Rhode Island, Vermont, www.neasc.org

North Central Association of Colleges and Schools, for Arizona, Arkansas, Colorado, Illinois, Indiana, Iowa, Kansas, Michigan, Minnesota, Missouri, Nebraska, New Mexico, North Dakota, Ohio, Oklahoma, South Dakota, West Virginia, Wisconsin, Wyoming, www.ncacihe.org

Northwest Association of Schools and Colleges, for Alaska, Idaho, Montana, Nevada, Oregon, Utah, Washington, www.cocnasc.org

Southern Association of Colleges and Schools, for Alabama, Florida, Georgia, Kentucky, Louisiana, Mississippi, North Carolina, South Carolina, Tennessee, Texas, Virginia, www.sacs.org

Western Association of Schools and Colleges, for American Somoa, California, Hawaii, Guam, Trust Territory of the Pacific, www.wascweb.org

Analysts and Experts

AberdeenGroup, conducts an IT market analysis that measures the buying intentions of IT executives for 35 application software categories and 11 technology infrastructure sectors, www.aberdeen.com

comScore Networks, researches consumer behavior on the Internet, www.comscore.com

Delphi Group, custom research and strategic consulting in emerging technologies, www.delphigroup.com

Eduventures.com, specialist in education research, www.eduventures.com

Employee Benefits Research Institute, a nonprofit, nonpartisan research organization to advance public knowledge of the importance of employee benefits to the economy, www.ebri.org

Ewing Marion Kauffman Foundation, conducts research that defines what it takes to be a successful entrepreneur; studies best practices for supporting entrepreneurship and its role in the country's economy; and supports organizations and institutions that help entrepreneurs, www.emkf.org

Forrester Research, identifies and analyzes emerging trends in technology and their impact on business, www.forrester.com

Gartner Viewpoint, educational arm of broad-based qualitative and quantitative data researcher, www.gartner.com

Goodmind, market research firm using online research for competitive advantage, www.goodmind.net

IDC Learning Services, worldwide researcher of education markets, www.idc.com

InsightExpress, online market research of technology markets, www.insightexpress.com

In-Stat/MDR, research in a number of high-tech markets, www.instat.com

Market Data Retrieval, provides mailing lists, database marketing services, state-by-state school directories, and statistical reports and analysis about the education market, www.schooldata.com

Nielsen//NetRatings, conducts an Internet audience measurement service, tracking the entire spectrum of Internet user behavior in 22 countries worldwide, representing nearly 90 percent of the global audience universe, www.nielsen-netratings.com

NPD Group, conducts point-of-sale research for a broad range of consumer products, www.npd.com

Certification

CompTIA, a global, 13,000-member IT trade group developing certification standards and best practices, www.comptia.org

Institute for Certification of Computer Professionals, nonprofit group dedicated to the establishment of professional standards in the computer industry, www.iccp.org

International Association for Continuing Education and Training, nonprofit association certifying providers of continuing education and training programs, www.iacet.org

International Information Systems Security Certification Consortium a nonprofit organization providing security practices training and certification to information security professionals worldwide, www.isc2.org

Government Agencies

Bureau of Labor Statistics, part of the Department of Labor, measures nationwide labor and occupational trends, www.bls.gov

Census Bureau, a good source of demographic information, www.census.gov

Department of Education, cabinet-level department devoted to educational issues and research, www.ed.gov

National Center for Education Statistics, the primary U.S. federal agency for collecting and analyzing data on education worldwide; provides an extensive list of statistical tables, charts and studies reporting on the condition and progress of education, nces.ed.gov

Sallie Mae, a government-sponsored enterprise that's the primary funder of federally guaranteed student loans originating under the Federal Family Education Loan

Program; its site contains comprehensive information and resources on financial aid, www.salliemae.com

Small Business Administration, a source of possible funding and plenty of useful information for the small-business person, www.sba.gov

Social Security Administration, projections on demographics, www.ssa.gov

Magazines and Newsletters

Certification Magazine, a monthly magazine covering the certification market, www.certmag.com

Education Week, published by the nonprofit Editorial Projects in Education, provides K-12 educators with local, state and national news, www.edweek.org

E-learning Magazine, a monthly magazine covering e-learning and especially corporate training, www.elearningmag.com

eSchool News, a monthly newspaper to help K-12 decision-makers use technology and the Internet to achieve educational goals, www.eschoolnews.com

ITWorld, a collection of newsletters, white papers, IT news, and Webcast sites published by Accela Communications whose parent company is IDG, www.itworld.com

Professional Training Associates, publishes *Managing People at Work*, *The Office Professional*, *Staffing Now* and *Every 1 Counts*, career-boosting newsletters for managers and office professionals, www.protrain.com

Technology & Learning Magazine, a publication for early adopters of technology in education, www.techlearning.com

The Chronicle of Higher Education, weekly news source for college and university faculty members and administrators, www.chronicle.com

The Complete K-12 Newsletter, produced by Education Market Research, specializes in K-12 school/library market research, www.ed-market.com

T.H.E. Journal, magazine and newsletters offered by T.H.E., an association for educators, www.thejournal.com

Training Magazine, a professional development magazine that advocates training and work force development as a business tool, www.trainingmag.com

Workindex.com, newsletter produced by the publishers of Human Resource Executive in cooperation with Cornell University's School of Industrial Labor Relations; links to more than 4,000 workplace-related Web sites and offers HR news and tools, www.workindex.com

Software

This is a small sampling of hundreds of specialized tools; find more on search engines such as Yahoo! and Google.

Blackboard, e-learning software and services, www.blackboard.com

Business Plan Write, business plan software from Business Resource Software, www.brs-inc.com

Centra, enterprise learning and knowledge management suite that includes Web meetings and teleconferencing from Centra Software, www.centra.com

Macromedia Director MX, for creating streaming video clips that can be downloaded and run by Macromedia Player versions, from Macromedia, www.macromedia.com

Media Player, Windows video and audio player from Microsoft, www.microsoft.com

PlaceWare, real-time multimedia conferencing service for presentations and collaboration between thousands of people simultaneously using popular Web browsers and telephones, www.placeware.com

RealOne Player, video and audio player from RealNetworks, www.realnetworks.com

Resolution, from Ncompass Labs, work-flow-based document creation tool, www.ncompass.com

Saba Learning, an Internet-based learning management system from Saba Systems, a developer of human capital development and management solutions, www.saba.com

WebCT, e-learning software suites for higher education, www.webct.com

WebEx, carrier-class communication services enabling users to share presentations, documents, applications, voice and video spontaneously in a seamless environment, www.webex.com

Successful e-Learning Entrepreneurs

Sarah Chapman and Devin Williams, co-founders, Spry Learning, www.sprylearning.com

John Clemons, CEO, LearnKey Inc., www.learnkey.com

Leon Levy, director, business development, MiraCosta College, www.miracosta-.edu/commsvcs

Mike Russiello, president and CEO, Brainbench, www.brainbench.com

Joe Saari and Ed Harris, co-founders, Precision Information, www.precision-info.com

Stephen Shank, CEO, Capella University, www.capellauniversity.edu

Morten Sohlberg, CEO, Sessions.edu, www.sessions.edu

Trade Groups

American Association of Community Colleges, nationwide trade group for community colleges, www.aacc.nche.edu

American Association of Retired Persons, a nonprofit membership organization for people 50 and over, providing information and resources, legislative advocacy and other member services; publisher of *Modern Maturity* and *My Generation* magazines, www.aarp.org

American Association of School Administrators, a professional organization for more than 14,000 elementary and secondary educational leaders across the United States and overseas, www.aasa.org

American Council on Education, international membership organization devoted to adult and higher education issues, www.acenet.edu

American Distance Education Consortium, an international consortium of educators devoted to distance learning, www.adec.edu

American School Directory, an omnibus Internet site with information on K-12 schools nationwide, www.asd.com

Association for Computing Machinery, worldwide association of 75,000 members devoted to computing; a $99 annual subscription provides access to more than a million pages of IT-related content and 200 online training courses on the ACM portal, www.acm.org

American Society of Training and Development, U.S. chapter of a worldwide trade association for workplace learning, forming a world-class community of practice for 70,000 members in more than 100 countries, www.astd.org

K-12 School Networking Conference, annual networking event for K-12 educators featuring speakers, workshops and a tradeshow, www.k12schoolnetworking.org

National Venture Capital Association, trade association representing the venture capital industry with a membership of 400-plus VC firms and organizations that manage pools of risk equity capital, www.nvca.org

RTPnet, a nonprofit organization promoting electronic communication, www.rtpnet.org/comp

Society for Human Resource Management, association of human resource professionals, www.shrm.org

Society for Technical Communications, a 23,000-member organization including technical writers, editors, graphic designers, multimedia artists, Web and Intranet page information designers and others whose work involves technical communications, www.stc.org

United States Distance Learning Association, a consortium of organizations devoted to the proliferation of distance learning, www.usdla.org

Web Sites

Bisk University Alliance, consortium of e-learning colleges and universities, www.bisk.com

CareerExchange.com, extensive job search database with online conferencing and a "people-match" program, www.careerexchange.com

Continue2learn.net, more than 500 self-paced, real-time interactive training courses over the Internet, www.continue2learn.net

EducationToGo, college-oriented e-learning portal, www.ed2go.com

e-Learning Center, gives ideas, tips and solutions on how to sharpen your skills and increase your knowledge, regardless of profession, www.e-learningcenter.com

eLearningDepot, a catalog of more than 1,000 courses offering e-learning programs and certification training for businesses and individuals, http://elearningdepot.com

Find Computer Schools, an IT Web portal with a powerful database of IT certification training searchable by training type, topic, certification type, state, ZIP code, and numerous other parameters, www.find-computer-schools.com

Hostway, provider of Web hosting services and online business tools for small to medium-sized enterprises, supporting more than 100,000 Web sites worldwide, www.hostway.com

HR.com, information, resources, products and services for individuals in human resource management, www.hr.com

NicheBoards.com, an alliance of 11 leading niche employment Web sites to help narrow your search for instructors and other workers, www.nicheboards.com

Oracle University, Web portal with training, certification information and other resources for the broad set of computer tools produced by Oracle, www.oracle.com

Orbis Online, develops reverse auctions for competitive bidding on products and services, www.OrbisOnline.com

Selling to Schools, a resource center for educational technology professionals, www.sellingtoschools.com

TechTutorials.com, a directory of almost 2,000 free computer tutorials and whitepapers, www.techtutorials.com

The TradeShow Coach, includes articles, books, tapes, workshops, and free weekly e-mail tips to help you get the most out of your trade show experience, www.TheTradeShowCoach.com

University of Phoenix, very large online educational institution, www.phoenix.edu

WorkSpace Resources, online source for information about the working environment, ergonomics, design and the contract furniture industry, www.workspace-resources.com

World Wide Learn, Web portal providing an independent directory of educational services and resources as well as hundreds of e-learning courses in 144 subject categories, www.WorldWideLearn.com

Glossary

Accreditation: recognition by an authorized standards-setting body—trade, governmental, or quasi-governmental—that a company is passing on a body of knowledge in a format that meets widely agreed upon educational standards

Asynchronous e-learning: self-paced courses, usually delivered online or through CD-ROMs, that enable students to take a course at the time and place of their choosing independent of the participation of an instructor or other students

Certification: acknowledgement that a student has successfully completed a course of study—usually, measured by passing an examination—that prepares him or her to work in a specific field or with a specific technology

CGI scripts: small programs that transfer a Web page visitor to another page when a hyperlink is selected

Course Management System (CMS): a software environment for developing, delivering, and administering courses; see also *Learning Management System*

CPM: cost-per-thousand impressions; the minimum number of ad views against which advertising rates are applied

Demographic category: a broad demographic characteristic or classification—for example, gender

Demographic target: the specific values or segments within a demographic category—males is one target within the gender category

Distance learning: Any course—synchronous or asynchronous—in which the student learns at a different time or place than the instructor; it's most often used to refer to learning over the Net but can also include books, satellite TV, videotapes, CD-ROMs, and even audio

Distance learning aggregator: creator of a Web site with the offerings of multiple e-learning organizations

Domain: a collection of Web pages associated with a unique domain name registered with one of the authorized registrars—for example, yahoo.com

HTML: Hypertext Markup Language; the coding language widely used to describe Web pages

Java: a compact but powerful scripting language originally launched by Sun Microsystems for creating small applets for the Net and now used very widely

Just-in-time training: an e-learning comparison to the just-in-time (JIT) delivery of manufacturing components by suppliers; for example, taking a quick course on Excel macros to complete a project, or, on a larger scale, taking an IT certification course to enable an individual to complete a project

LMS: Learning Management System; a full-service software environment that contains an extensive set of learning tools, which may include synchronous and/or asynchronous course presentation, various conferencing options, data storage and bulletin board services for students, administration tools, and many other services

Multiple revenue streams: recognizing the seasonality or cyclical nature of most markets, having revenue from more than one activity or class of customers; an example would be selling e-learning courseware to corporations as well as governmental and educational institutions

Page views: the number of times a Web page has been seen

Streaming media: multimedia sent over the Net in a "stream" rather than in a single file

Synchronous e-learning: courses delivered over the Net to multiple students simultaneously at a specified time

Top level domain: a group of Internet domains that end with a common suffix—such as .com, .net, or .edu—managed by a single domain registrar under the authority of the Internet Corporation for Assigned Names and Numbers (ICANN)

Unique audience: Internet advertising metric measuring the number of individual people that have gone to a site at least once during the defined time period

Vendor-neutral certification: IT certification examining a student's knowledge of generalized technology, such as local-area networking, rather than a specific vendor's implementations of that technology

Vendor-specific certification: IT certification examining a student's qualifications to work with a specific vendor's technology

Virtual private network: technology that creates a private, secure tunnel through the public Internet; it can connect multiple sites or individuals, and allow them to communicate, collaborate, and share files securely

Voice-over IP: transferring voice calls over an Internet connection using Internet Packet (IP) protocols, rather than over the landline or cellular telephone networks

Web site: a registered Internet domain or collection of domains using one or more unique URLs operated by a single entity

Whiteboard: an Internet variation on a longtime computer technology and a part of many LMSs, it provides for content displayed on one PC to be simultaneously displayed on other Internet-connected PCs

XML: Extensible Mark-up Language; a data description standard that is the successor to HTML that is much more programmable and permits greater interaction with databases

Index

A

Accountant, 74, 85
Accreditation for your e-learning business, 76–78, 143–144
Advertising
  direct mail/e-mail, 130
  expenses, 85
  on education portals, 124
  on your own Web site, 127
  search engine, 124
  selecting the right vehicle for your, 122–123
Angel investors, 112, 114, 116, 136
Appendix, 143–150
Application point of view *vs.* vendor bias, 53
Armed services. *See* Military
Assessment methods, improved, 108
Attorney, 73–74, 85

B

Brainstorming for a business/market idea, 15, 20–21

Branding, 72–73
Broadband technology, advantages of, 41
Brokerage services, 24–25
Budgeting basics, 79–88
Business
  education programs in workplace/home/college campus, 45–46
  idea, 15, 20–21
  model, possibility of "trumping" your original, 139
  skills training, growth of, 9
  structure, choosing your, 73–74
Business plan, 75–76, 113
  competitions, 115, 116
  financial statement as component of, 118
  software, 116, 118

C

Call center personnel, 51
Canned courses, 46, 97–98. *See also* Course content and delivery

CD-ROMs
  annual updating of, 3
  children's, 61
Certification for IT professionals
  components of, 52–53
  exams, 22
  infrastructure for, 24
  list of, 58
  providers, 11, 21–24
  standards, 145
  through independent exams, 53
  vendor course materials, 93
  vendor Web site, 125
  vendor-neutral *vs.* vendor-specific, 23–24
Chat rooms, 106–107
Children, e-learning market for educating, 8–9, 60–61. *See also* Schools
College market, 13, 31–38
  adult learners/back-to-schoolers, 35–36
  computer/Internet savvy generation, 33–34
  distance learning programs, 65

employer underwriting of adult learners, 33, 36
Internet use, 34–35
military, 36
supplementing a degree, 2–3
tuition, 33
working students, 36
Commercial office start-up expenses, 85–87
Community college online offerings, 64–65
Competition, researching your, 18, 54, 136
Conferencing services, 105
Consulting services, 25
Corporate
employees, ongoing training courses for, 3
employer underwriting of continuing education, 33
employment skills testing, 11
market's embrace of "distance learning," 4
market, 2
markets, outlook for e-learning segment, 9
training, 39–47
training expenditures by U.S. companies, 44
workers, professional niches, 42
Course content and delivery
application point of view *vs.* vendor bias, 53
as collaborative effort, 92
creating your own, 94–95
customized for client company, 46–47
e-learning, 89–95
e-learning, synchronous vs. asynchronous, 97, 105
e-learning, text and streaming media, 96, 105
experiential, 91, 95–96
linked to support components, 104
noncredit continuing education, 62
provider/publisher, 10
reselling or repurposing, 11, 92–94
Course management systems, 31, 37–38
features of, 106
start-up, 136–138

Course titles, examples of online, 55
Customer
referrals as best advertising, 130, 137
service as first priority, 130–131
support Web sites, 47

D
Database Administrator (DBA) certifications, 58. *See also* Certification for IT professionals
Delivery
of content, 90, 92, 95–99, 104–104
platforms, 104 (*See also* Course content and delivery)
Demographic research, 17
course using geographical mapping software, 47
Department of Defense
SCORM (Shareable Content Object Reference Model), 104
security needs, 57
Direct mail/e-mail advertising, 130
Directory services, 24–25
Domain name, registering your, 70, 72
dotcom failures, 80–81
DVDs, 108

E
e-books, 109
e-commerce courses, 43
e-learning
business resources, listing of, 143–150
categories of, 10–11
courses, direct consumer sales of, 47
distance, 31
diverse course/subject offerings of, 5
entrepreneurs, 24–26
in tandem with classroom teaching, 5
industry overview and long-range outlook, 8
initiatives as strategic component of business environment, 45
investments, preserving, 105
lifelong, 59–65
mainstreaming of, 44

searches, 125
ten technologies that promise to enhance, 108–109
your role in, 5–6
e-mail
advertising, 130
communication, 43, 105
newsletters, 128
Ebay, 26
Education
and e-learning, 7
and impact of Internet upon, 4
industry, overlap of market segments in, 8–9
market conversion to e-learning markets, 10
Elderly population, markets for expanding, 62–64
Elevator pitch, refining your, 113, 114
Employee
-to-employee interaction, 106
retention, 13–14
technical support, 51
training, ongoing courses for corporate, 3
training, outsourcing, 42
Enrichment and enjoyment, personal learning for, 9
Entrepreneurial
research findings, 134, 135
successes, 133–141
traits, 140–141
Entrepreneurs
and a can-do attitude, 107
successful e-learning, 147
Escrow companies, 26
ESL courses, 46
Exam preparation site, 11
Exit strategy, 114
Expert systems, 108
Experts, listing of, 144–145

F
Financial statement as business plan component, 118
Financing, 111–119
Financing, course, 26
Freelance
contractor, 11
writers and designers, hiring, 94
Friends and family financing, 112

G
Glossary, 151–153
Government agencies, 145–146

Graphic designers, hiring free-lance, 94

H

Handheld computers, 102
 and mobile phones as plat-forms with growth potential, 108–109
Homebased business, 82–85
 office set up, 83–84
 start-up expenses, 83
Home-based learning/working, appeal of, 6, 40, 41
Home-schooling market, 12, 30, 38
Hype, avoiding industry, 9–10

I

Idea
 capital, e-learning provider's role in supplying raw materials for, 5
 creating a unique business, 20–21
Income levels based upon educational attainment, 3
Incorporating your business, 74
Information (IT) professional
 long-term view, 50–51
 training, 49–58 (*See also* Certification for IT professionals)
Information security training, 50–51
Infrastructure provider, 10–11
Instant messaging (IM) growth of, 43, 106–107
Instructor
 beyond the, 92
 learning curve for, 105
 led continuing education courses, 62
 led online learning provider, 10
 the "credentialed," 98–99
 with academic/business back-ground, 46
Insurance needs, 76, 88
Intellectual property, protecting your, 99
Interaction, student-student and student-teacher, 105, 106
Interactive TV, 108
Interactivity as essential in e-learning, 45
Internet
 access, types of household, 41
 developer certifications, 58

explosion as seminal event for e-learning, 4
Investors
 "Angel," 112, 114, 116, 136
 as "data-driven," 43–44
 demanding and savvy nature of, 57–58
 development courses for, 56
 finding, 116
 IT professionals
 managerial courses for, 56
 profile of, 56–58
 profile of as potential student, 56
 tools for screening "pre-hire," 22
 training markets, growth of, 9

J

Job changing, Bureau of Labor Statistics data on current trend of, 5

K

Knowledge workers, e-learning offerings for, 42–43

L

Learning
 "just-in-time," 109
 management systems, 38
 styles, blending, 45
Legal help, 73–74, 85
Life-long
 e-learning, 59–65
 learning paradigm, 14
Limited liability company (LLC), 74
Listening skills, 139

M

Magazines, listing of industry related, 146
Market
 advantage, forging a, 17
 approach, determining the right, 16–17
 breakdown of e-learning, 8–9
 determining what motivates students in your chosen, 12
 opportunities, limitless nature of e-learning, 6
Market research
 checklist, 18
 Internet as vast resource for, 16
 preliminary, 15–16
Marketing, 122–131
 expenses, 85

merchandising as tool for effective, 131
 through vendor Web site, 125
Measurable goals, providing business customers with e-learning that provides, 45, 50
Microsoft
 co-ventures with, 137–138
 courses and certification, 3, 23, 52–53, 78
Middleman markets, 11, 24–26
Military market, 36, 57
Mission statement, 68–69
Moneymakers, computer courses as perennial, 43
More-with-less philosophy, 116–117
Multi-billion dollar market, e-learning as, 5

N

Naming your business, 70–72
 and your products and services, 70–73
 choosing and registering your domain name, 70, 72, 127
 "namestorming worksheet," 71
 registering fictitious name (dba), 74
Network Administrator certifications, 58
Network security courses, 51–52, 55
Newsletters, 146
Niche
 "within-niche" offerings, 61
 finding your market, 15, 19–26, 136, 138

O

Office equipment, tax deductions on purchase of, 80
Office space, subletting, 81
On site *vs.* off site training, 44, 46
On-the-job training, 13
Online forum, chat and message boards as student gathering places, 97, 105–106
Outsourced services, trend of, 42–43

P

Partnerships, business, 74
PayPal online escrow service, *26*
Perseverance, 115

Personalized learning, 108
Phoenix, University of, online degrees, 5, 32
Pricing
  examples of e-learning services and product, 17
  for certification courses, 24
  the product, 54–55
Professional associations
  meetings/seminars, 129
  networking through, 117
Programming skills, 56
Promotional expenses, 85
Public relations, 125–127
  expenses, 85
Public school market, 12. *See also* Schools
Purchasing decisions, teenage influence over technological, 60

R
Rainmakers, real-world, 115
Re-sellers, e-learning, 11, 93–94
Recruiters, 13
Referrals, customer, 130, 137
Regulatory requirements, business, 74
Remote workforce, growth of, 40
Results, e-learning that provides, 45, 50
Return on investment, 45
Revenue models (B2B/B2C), 24
Revenue streams
  developing multiple, 21
  generating alternate, 139–140
  self-funding, 117
Reverse Auction, 25

S
S corporation, 74
Sale, closing the, 139
Schools
  Bisk Education, 37
  college, 31–38
  course management systems, 31, 37–38
  elementary and secondary, 28–30
  funding for hardware, 28, 36
  learning management systems, 38
  public, private and charter, 12
  restrictive access policies, 29
  students and teachers, lack of computer skills, 28–29

Search engines, 124
Security professionals
  certifications, 58
  growth in field of credentialed, 51–52
Self-financing, 112
Self-funding revenue stream, 117
Seminars, improving upon traditional on-site, 44
Seniors, markets for expanding population of, 62–64, 126
Shoestring stage of your start-up, 118–119
Software, 147
  e-learning company, 101–109
  failures, 51
  for your business start-up, 84
  market for learning basics of, 62
  ongoing instruction, 43, 50
  simulations, 108
  training via Internet, 4
Sole proprietorship, 73–74
Standardized tests, prep for, 13
Start-up
  costs, 79–88
  strategies, 19–26
Strengths, determining your, 15
Students
  financing services for, 26
  gathering places, forums, chat rooms, message boards, instant messaging, 97, 105–106
  needs, determining, 12
Successful entrepreneurs, start-up stories of, 133–141
Support structure, Web as "giant," 15
Synchronous *vs.* asynchronous e-learning courses, 97

T
Talents, making best use of your, 107
Taxes, paying your business, 74
Technical difficulties, 14
Technologies that promise to enhance e-learning, 108–109
Technology, keeping up with changes, 14, 50–51
Teenage
  influence over purchase of technological devices, 60
  Internet cafe, 29
Telecommuters market, 40, 41
Testimonials, posting customers', 26, 137

Time and space, conquering through e-learning, 14
Titles, common online course, 55
Tools for the creative process, 104–105
Trade
  groups, 148
  shows, 129–130
Trademark, registering your, 72, 73
Traffic
  analysis, Web site software for, 123
  monitoring Web site, 26
Travel in post 9/11 world, 44

U
University market, 8–9, 13, 31–38. *See also* College market

V
Vendors, big name, 44
Venture capital, 81, 112–113, 114
Videoconferencing, 108

W
Web
  address, creating a memorable, 70
  advertising, 123–125
  aggregator, 11
  banner ads, 123, 124
  developers, 56
  page design courses, 43
Web site
  as advertising and PR vehicle, 127
  as your electronic business card, 85, 102
  creating a "sticky," 128, 131
  design and hosting expense, 88
  design, do-it-yourself, 107
  examples of Neilsen's weekly top 25, 127
  hosting, 88, 103
  linking yours to related sites, 127
  list of e-learning related, 149–150
  tools, 102–103, 104–105
Wi-Fi, 109
Wireless networks, evolving, 109
Word-of-mouth advertising, 130
Workplace as electronic information warehouse, 43
Writers, hiring freelance, 94